THE ONLY PATH

A Memoir

Dick Dorworth

Published by BookLocker.com, Inc., St. Petersburg, Florida.

Printed on acid-free paper.

BookLocker.com, Inc.
2017

First Edition

Dedication

For Jeannie

Table of Contents

BOOK ONE

Chapter I
THE GIFT

"All happy families are like one another; each unhappy family is unhappy in its own way."
Leo Tolstoy

"Sherman made the terrible discovery that men make about their fathers sooner or later....that the man before him was not an aging father but a boy, a boy much like himself, a boy who grew up and had a child of his own and, as best he could, out of a sense of duty and, perhaps, love, adopted a role called Being a Father so that his child would have something mythical and infinitely important; a Protector, who would keep a lid on all the chaotic and catastrophic possibilities of life."
Tom Wolfe

When father was 69 and I 47 he gave me an unexpected, priceless gift, the key to better understanding him and his life, and, therefore, me and mine. It was his birthday, July 5, 1985, and I suspect his gift to me he viewed as mine to him. He was that kind of man. Since a few years after his wife, my mother, died in 1971 Dad had lived a nomadic life out of a trailer he hauled around western America. He was visiting me in Ketchum, Idaho that summer and came to my tiny apartment where I'd arranged a small birthday gathering of a few old friends. He arrived a couple of hours early and I told him there were things I'd always wanted to ask but never had, details of

1

his life and our family's personal dynamics that were never clear to me, issues never discussed, things about which I was curious. I told him I'd like to turn on my tape recorder and tape him, and would he like to do that?

Dad's reply mirrored his life. "No," he said, "I wouldn't like to do that. But I will.........for you."

His gift was that tape and the conversations between us that grew out of it and the understandings I gained from them. Those insights were the keys to a couple of heavy trunks of angry baggage I'd carried around since childhood. Most people I know have questions, misperceptions, mysteries, unresolved angers and fears, and matters of simple curiosity about their family, especially parents, which have never been brought to the surface. The unasked question is the crucible of fear and ignorance. Many people live entire lives making fearful decisions and uninformed judgments based on attachments to childhood (and childish) misperceptions that came from Mom and Dad. Perhaps you, esteemed reader, know someone who is sleeping through life on a soft mattress of incomplete and puffed up information without acknowledging the sharp rock of instinct underneath, poking into dreams and psyche, dictating uncomfortable, painful and bent positions that denial and confusion term normal.

It requires an adventurous adult offspring to ask a parent for knowledge about matters not entirely comfortable. It takes a courageous parent to answer honestly. Adventure is more complicated, wide ranging and subtle than sailing unknown seas, scaling difficult mountains, jumping off high bridges with a bungee cord attached to the ankles, or, of course, leaping into the greatest adventure of them all---falling in love. All adventure is impelled by a search for truth which is found only at the risk of expanding and thereby changing understanding. Every exploration into the unknown is perilous. It is the intention of the seeker as much as the magnitude of risk, not the success or failure of the ultimate outcome that determines the value of the enterprise. The closer one gets and stays to truth, the deeper and more satisfying are the adventure and its lessons. Every adventurer seeks to know him or her self through the connection made by exploring, experiencing and expanding the limits of the known world. It is on the edge of such expansion that life is lived to its fullest and the most information found and exchanged. This instinctive, experiential insight was given scientific validity and definition in 1987 by a group of scientist who called it "Self Organized Criticality" or SOC.

By 1985 Dad was in the late stages of a nervous disease that caused him to walk, talk and appear to the uninitiated as if he were drunk, but he was not. A toxin picked up during World War II on Guam in the Pacific theatre (see "The Island of the Color Blind" by Oliver Sacks) had attacked his central nervous system, though he died without learning the source of his ailment. Embarrassment and frustration made this already reserved though friendly and kind man cautious about speaking to anyone at length. He was difficult for the inexperienced person to understand, never knew when his foot wouldn't land where his brain told it to go, and was in constant danger of choking while swallowing. Dad learned to choose his words carefully, to walk with the attention of a Buddhist monk, and to eat only small bites of soft, easily swallowed food. Still, his bald head perpetually displayed scabs and scrapes and his body was always bruised from the falls he took daily.

One of the things I asked was to explain a couple of photographs he had sent me some months before in the midst of other family memorabilia. They showed him as a young man in World War II military uniform in the company of a young woman I'd never seen. She was pretty and they were obviously happy. A demeanor of delight and enthusiasm shone in my father's face from those old photographs. I had never seen that look in his person. The uniform meant that he was married to my mother and I was at least four years old. I never saw him smile like that in the company of Mom. My parents had an unhappy and contentious relationship, drenched in alcohol and psychic discomfort; but I had never known Father to be unfaithful. He treated Mom with dutiful if uninspired fairness and responsibility. It was clear that neither of them really wanted to be where they were. I loved them both but hated their interactions, Mother's alcoholic bitchiness as well as Dad's resigned acceptance. Their dynamics, like those of all parents, had a huge impact on me, and at an early age I made a self-fulfilling promise to myself that I would never live like them or stay in such a sad, unrewarding relationship, a vow I managed to fulfill in spades at great and unforeseen cost to my life and the lives of those I most love. At the time of the interview I had just gone through my fourth divorce and my own personal life was in shambles. Who was the woman in the photograph, I asked? What was the story that made him smile in a way I never saw? And why had he sent those photos to me?

More than 40 years after he had last seen her, a ghost of happiness passed across father's face. He took his time before answering. The woman in the photo, Loreta, was the sister of his best friend in the military. Dad met her right after completing basic training, prior to being shipped to the Pacific theatre (and isn't it interesting we refer to war zones as 'theatres'?). Though we had subsequent conversations about her, some salient points of what transpired were never made clear. Loreta was married and had a child, just like Dad; but she and Dad fell in love and had an affair that, because of the war, could not have lasted very long. My mother knew about the affair, but I don't know if it was during or after the war that she learned of it. My knowledge of it certainly helped me understand and have more compassion for her behavior and aggressive disrespect toward her husband during my childhood and beyond. Dad's story was more complicated.

Dad loved Loreta and planned to divorce my mother and marry his love when the war was over.

Why hadn't they done that, I asked?

Loreta had suddenly and unexpectedly dropped dead of a heart attack while Dad was in the Pacific, managing a military warehouse on Guam. As he told me this more than 40 years later an ancient, unending hurt showed in his face. Some sorrows never heal and my father's abiding humanity was revealed as the source of his resignation, strength and kind generosity in the face of an adversarial marriage he did not want. After he heard about the death of his love, my father had a couple of years to agonize over his loss and to contemplate his post war path. The island of Guam in the Marianas of the South Pacific as a non-combatant in a bloody war was probably as good a place as any to mourn, but it seems to me that father never really recovered. He was never truly engaged or passionate about anything during the 50 years that I knew him. He was a kind and caring man, but denial was one of his primary coping mechanisms. Denial takes energy, and Dad simply didn't have enough left over for engagement.

After Loreta died Dad still intended to divorce Mom, but his friend, Loreta's brother, talked him out of it. He didn't have his love, his friend pointed out, but he did have a good woman and a young son waiting for him at home. From the perspective of a war time South Pacific Island, the depths of grief and the disappearance of passion, that must have seemed a decent, responsible, unfulfilling option. It was a place to go. So......he went. Father's name was Lee Alvin, and he was usually called

"Al," but some people knew him as Lee. Mom called him Al most of the time but switched to Alvin when she was angry, just as she called me "Richard" when annoyed with me. I have always wondered whether Loreta called Dad Al or Lee.

At some undetermined point Mom, whose name was Frances but was known to everyone as Fran, realized she was second choice in her husband's life. This could not have been acceptable to her. Rather than leaving him to seek her own options, she punished him for his betrayal for as long as she lived. It was the only place she had to go and they never made peace in that place, and their marriage was more a prison than a refuge. There is no more peace in prison than there is nature in a zoo. I was one of the inmates, and among the few things I knew for certain at an early age is that I wanted to break free. There is always a price for accepting the unacceptable, no matter how noble or generous the intention. In families that cost is distributed chaotically.

Until I was able to digest the meaning and effect on my life of my father's unexpected gift to me on his 69th birthday, I had at some subconscious level accepted that I deserved to be in prison for some unmentioned sin or quality or act of mine that could never be repaired. The first outward indication that some attitudes, angers and burdens of childhood were being shed was that I quit a lifetime habit of excessive drinking and drugging within two years of Dad's birthday interview. The shedding, like life itself, continues. Though this insight is admittedly self-administered pop-psychology, naturally I rebelled. And the rebel learns to thrive in unknown, unstructured territory, living like a warrior caught behind enemy lines, even, maybe especially, at home. The rebel is often and easily misguided, confuses friends with enemies and vice-versa, burns bridges to the past and future, and mocks both sacred cows and the sacred, but in the long run the rebel is freedom's best comrade and only hope. Dad was long dead before I understood that all my rebellions were only secondarily against society's strictures, my family's dysfunction, the dismal and transparent propaganda that pervades public education, and the narrow, proper, antiseptic people who give their lives to serving as wardens and guards, cooks and apologists, flaks and hit men for the prison. My resistance was primarily against the dangers of resignation and acceptance of the hypocrisy that is the status quo and stability of society. The world needs stability, but it also needs and will have resistance, movement and change. The status quo is entropy. Rebellion is chaos. The two states nourish the world like sunshine and rain. Early on I learned to love a good storm.

Every child carries the family dynamic around like a banner, a millstone, a set of standards or a secret wound, depending. Until the child understands that the dynamic was not created by him or her, that child's perspectives and options are limited, no matter how hard the rebellion, dutiful the acquiescence or deep the wound and resignation. While every parent has successes and failures, the very worst parent has the success of the child's existence. Several years before my father died, my friend Steve McKinney expressed his heartache, confusion and loneliness about his own biological father's rejection of him with these words: "Well, I know he was doing the best he could do with what he had to work with at the time." Though fundamental moralists disagree, Steve's words are a useful start to understanding and approaching the confounding emotions, dilemmas and actions of loved ones, including one's self.

My father's gift on his 69th birthday was not one he would have been able to offer me even a few years earlier. Nor would I have been ready to receive it. Still, it was a lovely gift of clarity, understanding and insight, three basic requirements of health, happiness and sanity.

Chapter II
THE WAR

"War cannot be justified, because--in terms of the rights of the species--it is worse than a crime. It is a waste."
Umberto Eco

"No country has suffered so much from the ruins of war while being at peace as the American."
Edward Dahlberg

The bomb. The atomic bomb. Fat Man. Little Boy. Hiroshima. Nagasaki. The Enola Gay. Victory. The end of World War II. Dad was one of the lucky ones who got to come back to the United States to face the reality of his post war path. History has termed my father's "the greatest generation" of Americans because it won a war that needed winning. Without demeaning the sacrifices, nobility or honor of that generation, the larger truth is that the reality of war is so grotesque and destructive that only generals, self-serving politicians and history can give it nobility, honor, justification or meaning, however contrived and incomplete its story. History is told by those who claim victory, but the only true winner in war is war itself. Victors and vanquished alike are victims. It is not only warriors and the civilians in their way who are damaged and destroyed by combat, for those who stay behind are injured and shattered in ways both obvious and hidden. The strands that weave together the fabrics of relationships, community, society and humanity are shredded and torn, discolored and rotted by the ethics and sordid reality of war. Hiroshima and Nagasaki left the specter of a mushroom cloud always roaming between the unconscious, subconscious and consciousness of America. I can report on my own, but I cannot imagine and am not qualified or worthy to contemplate the subconscious of the Japanese people, especially those who survived Hiroshima and Nagasaki. Those bombs ended World War II, but whether they were necessary to ending the war is a matter that deserves far more discussion and historical insight than it has ever received. It is my opinion they were neither necessary nor justified.

There is no audience to war. Everyone and everything are participants. I was three years old when WWII began, and most of my early memories are of the war. A few memories precede it, most of them of Reno, where I was born, and Pyramid Lake in northern Nevada where we lived as the only white family on the Paiute reservation while Dad worked on the highway between them. They include a near drowning experience in the waters of Pyramid Lake, from which I was saved by a collie bitch, Alice, owned by one of the Paiute families who were our neighbors. I remember the pounding waves of alkaline water and sand and Alice pulling me by the shirt onto the beach and the bosom and generous arms and sounds and sweet smells of a Paiute woman who held and comforted me while I sobbed and coughed up alkaline water. (Or is the memory only the remembrance of the re-telling of the story as I grew up? Where was Mom? Where was Dad?) This is a memoir, words composed from the haphazardly organized contents of the warehouse of memory. Both reader and writer must remember (sic) that memory itself is as imperfect as humankind, William Faulkner's insight that "The past isn't dead, it isn't even past," needs tempering. I think of Barbara Kingsolver who wrote in "Animal Dreams," "It's surprising how much memory is built around things unnoticed at the time," and "Memory is a complicated thing, a relative to the truth, but not its twin." A memoir is written and needs reading in and is relevant to the present more than the past. The incident was my first near death experience, the proverbial straw that caused Mom to insist that Dad quit the only decent job he could get in that depression era economy and move back to Reno to work in a gas station for not quite enough pay to get by. Mom was also disconcerted that my first language was Paiute which I spoke more fluently with the other children and parents of Pyramid Lake than I did with her in English. (I don't recall a word of Paiute now, alas.) I don't know that Mom was or was not a racist, but she was highly distrustful and frightened of people who were in any way different from her small circle of friends, family and experience. She was easily threatened and so far as I know Mom never had a friend or close acquaintance that was not white. She certainly had none among the good Paiute women of Pyramid Lake where the stark, lovely, empty desert landscape more clearly delineated her loneliness among indigenous Americans. Another pre-war memory is of father wearing a Santa Claus hat at Christmas. He is Christmas drunk happy and beating a toy drum (a Christmas present for me?), and he beats the drum and beats the drum and breaks the drum and I am crying. Another time I ate several of my mother's cherished cigarettes and vomited them up and was sick with tobacco poisoning long enough for it to take root in my unconscious so that smoking, which eventually killed Mom the slow, hard way through emphysema, was one of the few popular vices I completely avoided in the over long process of growing up. To this day I detest the smell of cigarette, cigar and even marijuana smoke, whether fresh and floating in the dying air or imbedded in the walls, furniture, rugs and curtains of rooms and restaurants, bars and cars. Eating Mom's cigarettes was one of the best things I did as a toddler, though, like other unpleasant lessons in life it was some time before its salutary influence was appreciated. Fate will have its way, and parents--no matter how good or bad, negligent or caring--are the cornerstone of each child's destiny. Mom, whatever her conscious intention in the matter, steered me clear from her vice without really meaning to, a gift and a blessing for which I have become belatedly grateful.

Once World War II started my family unit came unraveled in myriad ways, some of which I would not recognize for more than 40 years. Those who champion family values out of one side of their mouths and war out of the other are absurd, champions of the oxymoronic, willing to fight (or, in all too many cases, to send their children and the children of others to wage war) offensively to the death in defense of schizophrenia. Dad joined the military and went away to be trained and meet Loreta and find the best if short lived happiness of his life. Mom and I stayed in Reno where she sold tickets for the Greyhound Bus Company. She also volunteered with the USO, as did hundreds of thousands of American women whose men had gone off to fight in the Pacific and Europe and Africa. As a result, there were a succession of strange men in uniform for dinner in our house and walks in the parks of Reno by the Truckee River and large picnic gatherings of boys and young men, celebrating their lives before vanishing into war. It was a last flash of patriotic recreation in the company of young women, many of them married to men who had already left, including my mother. One of these functions took place at Bowers Mansion, between Reno and Carson City in the Washoe Valley rain shadow of the Sierra Nevada. It was an appropriate place for a recreational outing for Nevada warriors of the 20th century. Eighty years earlier it had been built by Sandy Bowers, one of the new multi-millionaires of Virginia City's silver rich Comstock Lode which Abraham Lincoln had used to finance the Union side of the Civil War in exchange for an early and easy inclusion of Nevada into that union. Bowers spent the unheard of (in 1863) sum of nearly half a million dollars on the Scottish style stone mansion complete with lawns, gardens, swimming pools and fountains looking across the valley to the silver-laden desert hills that had bankrolled it. He built it to please his Scottish born pauper wife, but within a few years Bowers had died and his wife fell on hard times and lost the mansion. By the time of World War II it was owned and operated as a resort by a man named Ritter. Another early near death experience took place in one of the Bowers Mansion swimming pools during a USO function. For reasons now forgotten, Mom wanted to leave the party and I did not, an early indication of the dynamic that dominated our relationship--Mom trying to manipulate and drag me one way, and me resisting and running in any other direction. She grabbed me by the arm, as impatient, frustrated and overwhelmed mothers often do with recalcitrant children, probably accompanied with unkind words of threatened retribution for my disobedience. It seems likely I intuited early on that Mom wasn't really on my side in the struggles of life. I tore loose from her grip and raced away as fast as my four year old legs would move to the edge of the swimming pool and beyond. I leapt into the pool and, since I couldn't swim, sank immediately to the bottom. Mom, who couldn't swim either, stopped at the edge of the pool. She was likely filled with a hysterical mixture of rage, fear and helpless desperation that was to mark the moods of her entire life, especially with her husband and son, the bookends of her personal disappointments. Mom never had it easy in her family life. It is not hard to imagine her feelings and the urgency with which she called for help from the recreating warriors to be.

Peace and calm, satisfaction and safety filled my spirit as the water filled my lungs on the bottom of the Bowers Mansion swimming pool. It was beautiful down there, quiet, sensuous and, most important, free. For a short amount of time I was supremely happy and would gladly have stayed in that place forever. Unfortunately, like all moments of deep human happiness and the illusion of freedom, it couldn't and didn't last long. It had been millions of years since my system had gills and my evolved system began sucking water instead of oxygen and I passed out. There is no human happiness without oxygen.

I woke with a sailor straddling me and pumping water out of my lungs while I coughed and cried, and the sailor wasn't nearly as comforting, sweet smelling or generous as the Paiute woman at Pyramid Lake the last time I'd heedlessly leapt into unmanageable waters.

In the early 1940s Reno, as the town slogan--"The Biggest Little City in the World"--indicates, was still a little city. The surrounding desert and mountain country was sparsely populated. The Truckee River drains Lake Tahoe of the mountains and empties its waters into Pyramid Lake in the desert. It runs through Reno west to east, dividing the city north to south, and is its defining geographic feature. Reno, the desert, the lakes Pyramid and Tahoe, the Truckee river and, most important, the mountains were the essential geographic features of my formative years. But there was a break during World War II when we left Reno and I lived in a series of boarding houses in Berkeley, Albany and Richmond on the urban east side of the San Francisco Bay of California. Mom worked for Greyhound Bus in Oakland and lived with two of her sisters in an apartment by Lake Merritt. I got to visit some weekends. At times she took me to movies. I missed her when I was at the boarding houses, and I believe she missed me, but there was always a discernable relief from a palpable tension at the end of our weekend reunions. I think now that Mom was doing her best to do what she thought was right, but the truth was that life had overwhelmed her. In addition to the normal frustrations in the life of a young woman with a high school education and no highly marketable skills, the war had taken her husband and bread winner, another woman had taken her man's heart, she had a son she wasn't sure she wanted and didn't quite know how to parent and she was sharing a small apartment with two other women while working a mindless job with no relief in sight.

One of those sisters, Aunt Motie, had a son, Cousin Peter, a year older than me who also spent the war in various bay area boarding houses. Motie was divorced from Peter's father who was mentioned not at all, as if he didn't exist in the past, present or future. In a certain sense, she was entirely successful in this suppression and pretense of her family dynamics. Peter never met his father. Aunt Motie seemed to me a stern, sad woman always a little pissed off at life, but she treated me with care and respect if not warmth. I loved those weekends when Peter and I got to visit our mothers at the same time. Peter was my best friend in those days, and it seems odd to me that our mothers never arranged to board us in the same place so we could have some family connection, companionship and comfort. Both Motie and Mom were dead before it occurred to me to ask why they hadn't done that. The other sister, Aunt Minnie, was a hard living spinster who loved me like a surrogate son and who eventually drank herself to death. Minnie, Motie and Mom were part of a huge family. Their father, Crawford Barkley, and his father, James Barkley, married sisters after James' first wife died; and then these two related families proceeded to have 21 children. This Barkley tribe often lived together. I was raised an only child and cannot imagine the family dynamics and convoluted relationships of the Barkley clan. In family lore, James' brother, Alben, was

Vice-President of the United States under Harry Truman, who, in the last analysis and hardest judgment was responsible for Hiroshima and Nagasaki. Alben was a lawyer and eloquent politician who stayed in Kentucky. James was a restless and eloquent atheist who left Kentucky as a young man to wander the west as a peripatetic preacher (yes), cattle rancher and hotelman. I have never been able to determine if James and Alben were really brothers or if they only shared the last name and James and family made a fake connection to a famous American. James seems to have always seen the big rock candy mountain and a better life just over the next horizon, and his three grand-daughters could have used some of his hopefulness as they endured World War II and its aftermath.

Mom and Minnie tended to confront the chaotic, catastrophic possibilities and realities of life head-on with copious amounts of alcohol. They were best friends, alcohol was one of their bonds and in the Lake Merritt days they were young enough that extreme social drinking was still fun and relaxing. It later followed the predictable, traditional course of hideous and destructive behavior. I wasn't around, but one of the stories the family liked to tell was the night Aunt Minnie passed out in her Oakland apartment with a lighted cigarette in her hand. She burned the apartment to a crisp and got some serious burns on her body before firemen carried her to safety. While Minnie's fire was part of family lore in my childhood, I don't know where her sisters were that night.

I was never mistreated, abused, disrespected or harmed in those boarding houses, but I hated them and missed my parents with a passion that has marked the major disappointments and times of sadness in my life. There is absurdity, impasse, even unresolved craziness in passion for absent people, things, places and times, but passion, however impractical and inconvenient trumps acceptance of the unacceptable---any time. One woman who kept care of me and four other boys in her Albany home insisted we call her "mother." Her name was Mrs. Siedenberg. I refused to call her anything but "Mrs. Siedenberg", such was my sense of loyalty and propriety, though the other boys called her "mother." One day my real mother came from Oakland to visit and take me away for the day from the Siedenberg home just below Albany Hill, covered with Eucalyptus trees where I spent my happiest hours playing with my fellow boarding house inmates or alone. Even now, 70 years later, the smell of Eucalyptus evokes in me a delightful reminder of relief from the oppression and loneliness of not living where and with whom I wanted. Mom came that day to take me to San Francisco to see a U.S. battleship (through perhaps it was a carrier or destroyer or some lesser weapon of war) returning from the Pacific. It isn't clear why she did that, but she was a patriotic sort who worked for the USO and sometimes took me to war films of the time (I still remember Robert Mitchum in "The Story of G.I. Joe" draped dead over a mule). Perhaps she wanted us both to believe that war was glorious, honorable and worth the aches, pains and confusion of shattering the family structure. Or maybe she knew something more, if only instinctively, and wanted me to get beyond the illusions of war. Whatever her reasons, the ship was a huge mass of bombed, strafed, and Kamakazied floating metal that was grotesque to my young imagination. The bridge was gone, the deck full of holes and undulations, the gun turrets irregularly spaced because some of them had vanished. There were giant, twisted shards of metal and mammoth, gaping molten holes like Rorsarch blots in steel. The ship listed. It was clear that something dishonorable and lacking in redemption had taken place in and around and because of that ship. I wish I knew the name of the ship and its history, but I do not. The experience gave me the realization without a vocabulary to describe it that anyone who saw honor or glory in that was crazy or a bullshitter. (A crazy bullshitter?) Mom and I were part of a large crowd. There was little talking. It was quiet. We all just looked.

Then we took the ferry back across the bay and Mom returned me to the boarding house in Albany and went back to her Oakland apartment and Minnie and Motie. My insides felt like that battleship looked. I've felt something like that a number of times in my life and it is not a good feeling. I associated that ship with the war and with my father being in the war. I was terrified for my father and that I might never see him again. I wished so hard that Father be okay that I came to believe that he would be. To do that I had to get through the ruined battleship feelings inside that scared me so badly that fear took on a life of its own as fear always does unless it is met head on, the sooner the better. Thus, without knowing its significance or truth, I began the lifelong process of dealing with fear as the first and most deadly enemy. Fear itself is far more dangerous and insidious than whatever inspires it.

After a longer time than a child has to spare waiting for the adult world to gain the peace and raise the children, Dad came home from the war in one physical piece. It was the happiest day of my young life to see Father intact after the war. He made it. (In actuality, he never saw combat and was in little danger of being shot or blown up for the entire war, but I didn't know that then.) He didn't come back like the battleship. He was unscathed so far as I could see, though as we all learned in the ensuing years war doesn't let anyone go home unchanged or without damage and scars. But he made it, and if he could get through a long war so could I. The natural duty of a son is to do as well as his father and better if he can, but World War II destroyed my father in myriad ways and the physical one would not appear for 20 years and not be understood for 40.

Chapter III
THE MOUNTAINS

"Take no one's word for anything, including mine--but trust your experience. Know whence you came. If you know whence you came, there is really no limit to where you can go."
James Baldwin

"Although mountains belong to the nation, mountains belong to people who love them."
Dogen

"All true paths lead through mountains."
Gary Snyder

The war ended. Father came back, if not home. The family reunited. I didn't have to live in the hated boarding houses any longer, though to this day I have a manifest nostalgia at the sight of Albany Hill and the smell of Eucalyptus. Being melancholy for a hated and lonely time and experience is one symptom of the complexity, contradiction and convolutions of human life and passions. If destiny is more than a crap game, if chaos disguises an order that we do not see, if we really are products of and producers of our own karma, then difficult times are those of the most growth and learning, and our nostalgia is the true reverence of respect for and acknowledgement of our paths through our inner Himalaya. At least so it seems and feels to me. Dad's happiness at being off Guam and back from the war must have been strongly flavored with self-imposed resignation. Mom's relief and happiness to have her husband back eventually (immediately?) was tinged with resignation wrapped in the bitterness of a marriage that had lost its heart to a dead woman. In all fairness, it is not entirely certain that mom was a model of faithfulness to her marriage during those war years. I never had the opportunity to sit her down with a tape and ask difficult questions that I am not convinced she would have honestly answered. During the war she sometimes took me on outings to parks, restaurants and an occasional movie in the company of men I didn't know and never saw again. Loneliness is the handmaiden of sorrow and the ghost of joy and whatever Mom's relationships with those men and whatever her reasons for including me on those outings, loneliness is a vacuum that needs filling, sorrow a specter that needs banishing. I was the only one in our family completely happy that we were together. I was literally and figuratively the glue that, for better and/or worse, held it together. Whether it was love, duty, stubbornness or resignation that kept them bound in a loveless pact, I love both my long dead parents and am grateful to them. They did the best they could do for me with what they had to work with at the time, for most of what they had was given with the best love they could muster. The best of it was wonderful and the worst of it was, viewed in retrospect from the knowledge gained in more than 70 years, not too bad and far better than what comes to most of the world.

Our first post WWII home was a tiny trailer in the small east bay community of Clayton, California. Uncle Harold, dad's severe alcoholic half-brother, had acquired some land there. It was a place to go. My parents needed some time and space to get reacquainted and figure out a direction in life and Harold was able to provide that. Only a few memories from that time remain, but they are clear and, one can assume, important signposts along a memoir.

The Barker family. The Barkers lived next door and I loved them. They had two children around my age, a boy and a girl, who were my friends. The Barkers were wonderful. They talked funny when they talked at all, dressed in bib overalls, were really skinny and seemed to me the most exotic, mysterious people I had ever known. The Barkers were migrant farm workers from Oklahoma. They were true "Oakies," the living embodiment of what John Steinbeck described in "The Grapes of Wrath," a Joad family named Barker who I loved for the reasons a young boy loves people he will never really know or understand, but it assuredly had something to do with the solidarity of their family. They were a unit, a glamorous species that had been everywhere, lived in a thousand places, followed the work and stayed together. The Barker kids had never lived in rooming houses with strangers, pressured to violate their loyalty to Mom and Dad, worried about whether Dad was coming home or what Mom was up to or, despite a thousand moves, slept in a stranger's home. When I couldn't live with my parents I missed them deeply, and when I got them back I unfavorably (and unfairly) compared them to the Oakies next door. Early in life the dynamic began that if Mom and Dad couldn't be happy with me then I wouldn't be happy with them, the root of all judgment. That the Barkers had a far more desperate situation and deeper problems to deal with than my own never occurred to me. They provided my first life experience of seeing the greener grass on the other side of the fence, a few decades before I heard the wisdom of Little Richard's perspective on the matter: *"The grass really may be greener on the other side of the fence, but it sure is hard to cut;."* and Bob Dylan's darker, more adult admonition, *"Don't go mistakin' Paradise for that home across the road."*

Making Mom and Dad laugh with my powers of observation. Somehow (the Barker kids?), I had learned the difference between a boy cow and a girl cow. The boy cow had a single long tapering growth hanging below his hind legs, the girl cow had a big balloon with bumps on it hanging below her belly. At some point I must have told them how I could tell the difference, and after that whenever we saw a cow they would insist, often for the benefit of friends who had not seen the performance, that I differentiate between the boy cows and the girl cows and explain how I knew. It never failed to elicit uproarious laughter from my parents and their friends who were of a sexually repressive era and culture and hypocritical set of values that my generation, not surprisingly, would shun and turn upside down. Whenever I see cattle in the golden fields of California I think of boy cows and girl cows and of the open-mindedness of an easy and innocent laugh.

Nails make tires go flat. Uncle Harold was a small florid faced man who was always good and kind to me but whom I avoided when possible because he was drunk much of the time and smelled awful all the time. I intuited an undefined menace in his lop-sided smile and halting gait. One day, for unremembered reasons, I booby trapped Harold's car with a series of 40 penny nails placed so that one or more of them would puncture a tire when the car was moved. The trap worked, flattening two tires. Harold came to me and asked if I'd done that. When I admitted to it he was kind and resigned and told me I'd done the right thing to tell the truth but that I made it hard for him and to please not to do it again. Dad, on the other hand, berated me and was furious in a way I had not seen. I liked Uncle Harold more than I had before I flattened his tires, and I became more guarded with Dad and with what I let him see, though he was only reacting to the reality that Harold could have and might have put us out at any time. Mom and Dad had enough problems without their son being a vandal and booby trapping their landlord, even if he was a half brother.

The most stark, clear, thrilling memory of that time was leaving Clayton and moving to Lake Tahoe in the Sierra Nevada on the Nevada/California border in 1946. Life without mountains has become as unimaginable to me as snowfall without cold. I was seven years old the day we drove into the Sierra and 70 years later I still have an image of stopping the car loaded with everything the family owned, which could not have been much, on Echo Summit near Tahoe's South Shore and breathing clean mountain air and seeing the most beautiful, exotic landscape imaginable. It was a springtime blue sky day with snow on the ground and freedom in the hills waiting for me to join her. My instincts spoke directly to my young soul, welcoming me home and telling me that whether I lived in a palace with loving family or a rooming house with strangers my home would always be in the mountains.

It was a gift, a mystery, a compass and a path for life as natural as breathing, as sure as the heart of love.

Chapter IV
LAKE TAHOE

"I played the wrong wrong notes."
Thelonius Monk

"....the inmost moving impulse in all true mountain-lovers, a feeling so deep and so pure and so personal as to be almost sacred--too intimate for ordinary mention. That is, the ideal joy that only mountains give--the unreasoned, uncovetous, unworldly love of them we know not why, we care not why, only because they are what they are; because they move us in some way which nothing else does...."
F. W. Bourdillon, as quoted by Sir Arnold Lunn

Lake Tahoe in the late 1940s was a paradise for the only child of a couple trying to put a life together from the wreckage of a structure that couldn't have been very sturdy even before the twin tornadoes of war and infidelity struck. But families do not always function according to the expectations placed upon them or in the dynamic patterns of what is loosely termed the nuclear family. Families are and families function and families get the job done, but not always along the path intended or imagined.

We went to Lake Tahoe because one of the family members had something going and needed workers to help him make it go. Harvey Gross had made some money during World War II illegally dealing in the officially rationed staples of booze and beef. He was an uneducated butcher with ambition, tenacity and a great love and devotion for his wife, Llewellyn, who was beautiful, intelligent, as exuberant as her husband was stolid and among my favorite people. Llewellyn was my mother's sister and she and Harvey had parlayed their black market booze and beef booty into a piece of property just inside the Nevada state line on Highway 50 by the Lake of the Sky, Lake Tahoe. The place became known as Stateline. That the property had been the site of a Presbyterian Church camp that Harvey and Llewellyn were turning into "Harvey's Wagon Wheel Saloon and Gaming Hall" was a metaphor lost or at least repressed by a group of people who had just survived a horrific war, were doing whatever they could to weave together the strands of their lives after that war and were thrilled and grateful to have something to do to support themselves in a mountain setting as beautiful and inspiring to the human spirit as the past several years had been degrading to it. Beneath it all they were adapting to the new reality of a changed world where time was relative and the atomic bomb gave official sanction to evil having a seat at the table of international diplomacy and politics until the end of time. It was not an environment conducive to contemplating metaphor, irony, consequences or the subtle shades of the moral colors of livelihood. It was a time to survive and to learn again to live. The first purpose of life is survival.

That's what we did.

Dad, a natural scientific intellectual who probably should have been a research chemist or a college professor, went to work in a succession of jobs connected to Harvey's empire building--carpenter, plumber, roofer, motel manager, twenty-one dealer, craps dealer, pit boss, money counter and book keeper. They were the trades of the rest of his life and the latter two defined his relationship with Harvey and determined the path of our lives. Mom worked as a cook and waitress and change girl in the casino. Along with Harvey and Llewellyn and various other aunts and uncles and cousins and an eclectic collection of characters who gravitated to the South Shore of Lake Tahoe in the post-war late 1940s, they became the pioneers of the burgeoning gaming/recreation industry that would mark and alter that most lovely body of water and its environs as nothing else in history. Their closest circle of friends were the bartenders, dealers, waiters, cocktail waitresses, pit bosses, bouncers, show girls and the assorted hustlers, card sharks, pimps, hookers and hangers on who always gravitate to industries of human weakness and social disintegration, in this case legal gambling, 24 hour a day drinking, legal prostitution and revolving door matrimony. These human/social/emotional activities are as integral and necessary to the fabric of human life as garbage dumps, sewage ponds, oil refineries and slaughter houses, but there are consequences for those who work in them, live next to them and raise their children within them.

The folks coped and I learned to maneuver through their coping mechanisms by using my own, primarily reading and wandering alone and sometimes with friends through the mountains of the mostly uninhabited landscape surrounding Lake Tahoe. Some of those excursions were expeditions including a goal, a proposed route, some food and water in a bag and an extra shirt or coat. While the concept of "adventure" was unknown to a young boy, the impetus to explore, to follow curiosity, to reach and see beyond the edge is innate, though such stimulus is sometimes threatening to and feared by the cautious, invested and powerful and it can be both trained and bludgeoned into conformity, incuriosity and blind faith. One summer day in 1950 or 1951 my buddy John Robinson and I had a day in the mountains that changed something--perspective, scale, possibility or maybe direction--inside. I knew it then and remember it now though details of the day are indistinct, and I never see that area of the

Sierra without smiling. The day stays in mind as the biggest of its kind in that pre-teen-age Tahoe time when summer rules and parental supervision started and ended with the admonition to be home for dinner. Whether it was trust and confidence in our basic instincts and capabilities or uncaring neglect of the duties of parenthood, the children of Tahoe in the post WWII era had a lot of latitude and a great deal of personal freedom, many years before I knew the difference between Mahatma Gandhi's practicality *"The greater our innocence, the greater our strength and the swifter our victory."* and William Blake's spirituality *"To see the world in a grain of sand, And heaven in a wild flower: Hold infinity in the palm of your hand, And eternity in an hour."* My folks probably thought I'd gone to the beach the day John and I headed to what we called Eagle Rock, a remote, romantic, mysterious outcrop visible high above and to the northeast of Kingsbury Grade, which went over the Sierra to Genoa, Nevada's first community. It seemed unreachable until we decided to reach it and it became a huge goal that gladdened our hearts from the moment we embarked. I was 11 or 12, John a year older, when we set off from South Shore along Highway 50 and up the narrow dirt road of Kingsbury, filled with our quest and the self-sufficient knowledge, even glee, that no one in the world knew where we were or what was our goal. After a couple of hours we veered off Kingsbury into unknown terrain of pine, fir, aspen and manzanita sprouting out of the sandy soil and dirt of the great Sierra Nevada under a clear mountain sky. We were guided by a general sense of direction and the pure joy of going where we had never gone before, secure in the knowledge that even as we plodded up, always up, with fatigue taking its toll on body and motivation, turning around and going down would eventually get us back to Tahoe, home, dinner. John was big for his age, always strong and athletic and a fine skier; we encouraged each other to continue in those times when we could see neither Eagle Rock nor Tahoe. The constants were the upward slope, the downward slide of our energies, our companionship and that ineffable something that had started us in the first place. We went on for hours and late in the day gained the ridge and scrambled up Eagle Rock on top of our Sierra Nevada world, the backyard of my childhood. To the east lay the Carson Valley and the high desert mountains of Nevada. To the west was the Tahoe Basin holding the Lake of the Sky, nature's own bassinette. Being on and looking around from the summit of Eagle Rock was the most exciting, wonderful thing I had ever done. We went back down and I made it home for dinner and never told my parents where we had gone. After that day I always knew solace and meaning were mine for the taking, always there to be explored and experienced in my own backyard, one step away from the highways and byways of civilization, no matter where I may be. It would be many years before I discovered, first in the writings of Muir, Thoreau, and Abbey and later with companions, that I was a member of a tribe, not a hermit of the spirit.

Mom was a voracious reader, mostly of pop trash detective novels of the Earle Stanley Gardner, Mickey Spillane, Agatha Christie genre, though she often read the best sellers of the day. Among her legacy to me is a love of reading, of literature, of the benefits, comfort and tools of life to be found in a good book. It has long intrigued me that she so often directed me to a higher standard of literature than she generally read. It was how a working woman with a high school education hoped and encouraged her son to a better life than her own. In that endeavor she was successful. I still have some of the hard bound books she gave me as a boy, including the "Essays of Michael de Montaigne", illustrated by Salvador Dali, "The Travels of Marco Polo," and, to illustrate her quirkiness,

"Archy and Mehitable." She got me "The Silver Skates" by
Hans Brinker and the stories of Jack London and everything by
Mark Twain before I was 12 years old. In those pre-TV days
on the south shore of Tahoe as the only child of heavy drinkers
who had trapped themselves in a contentious, dysfunctional
relationship, books were a savior, a refuge, a direction, and I
loved them.

And I loved Mom and Dad, but they could sure be problem
parents in those times when alcohol took them away from their
best selves and from all of me. I spent many nights in those
years waiting all night alone in the back seat of the various
family cars outside the clubs, casinos and bars of Tahoe, Reno,
Carson City and Las Vegas while Mom and Dad partied.
Sometimes it was cold. Always it was lonely. Sometimes it was
scary. And I always hated it. As often as not they drank until
dawn. I fought back in various ways, sometimes more
successfully than others. Once in Las Vegas after hours in the
car I was scared and convinced my folks had finally completely
abandoned me. I got out of the car (which I was told never to
do) and went to the door of the casino and found a bouncer,
told him my predicament and asked him to help me find my
parents. He did, bless him, becoming my immediate ally and
dressing down and embarrassing my mom and dad and their
friends in front of their drinking companions and assorted
denizens of pre-dawn Las Vegas night life. The bouncer kicked
them out of the casino with the warning to get me to a decent
bed and never come back to that casino. Mom and Dad were
furious but I didn't care, and I was too young not to care about
what my parents thought. Another time outside the bowling
alley at Tahoe's Stateline I got cold and tired of the
interminable waiting and I turned on the car headlights and
honked the horn until Dad came out and admonished me for
ruining everyone's good time. He gave me his coat, told me in

strong terms to quit honking the horn, and went back to the party. He didn't notice the headlights. I didn't honk the horn any longer, but the lights wore the car battery down by the early morning hours when they were ready to leave. It was a big problem for my thoroughly inebriated parents to get the car started and guide it home to Zephyr Cove, but I didn't care about their problem. I just wanted my own bed.

But best of all were the Sierra Nevada and Lake Tahoe which formed the matrix of the inner and outer landscapes of both my childhood and adult lives. John Muir referred to the Sierra Nevada as "the range of light" because of the reflected light of the sun in the clean, pure 19th century California air on its myriad granite domes and cliffs and slabs, many of them polished to a high sheen by glaciers, all of it smoothed and washed by millennia of snow and rain and runoff. Muir was a spiritual man and mountains were the ground of his belief, home of his cathedrals, altar of his devotion and realm of his best life. The Sierra Nevada, the range of light, was the source of Muir's illumination, as it was for me long after Muir was dead and years before I knew anything about illumination or the needs and mountainous grounds of the spirit and imagination. Early on the mountains and the lake became home and true refuge from the psychic battles being waged at home and in the social circles my parents joined. Those circles revolved around the casinos of Stateline and the people who worked in them. Some were relatives. Harvey and Llewellyn were owners, bosses, relatives and friends. They also included the shady and eccentric, criminal and colorful, opportunistic and ambitious, the damaged and adrift. The world of gambling is based on the economics of human weakness, not human need, and there are always consequences for the livelihoods we choose. The most morally/ethically/socially immature industries are usually governed and peopled by the conservative, the reactionary, the aggressively self-serving and least capable of abstract thought or the concept of social activism. There were card sharks and hookers and cowboys, ex-marines with murder and torment in their eyes, emigrants from the burgeoning streets of southern California with city smarts and ambition, people like Mom and Dad building a new life and a shelter from their own storms out of whatever tools they could find in the detritus of World War II, con-men and land sharks and (so it seems in hindsight) a plethora of alcoholics. My favorites were Bev and his wife, Van. His full name was Beverly Beverly and hers was Van Beverly. Just the names were exotic enough to catch the attention of a young boy with an ear for language. They were both straight out of a Damon Runyon story, true, real and wonderful, however disreputable according to certain upright standards of our culture. Bev and Van drank and socialized with my parents and taught me more than I had a right to know. Before I was 12 he was teaching me the basics of how to deal cards off the bottom and from the middle of the deck and how to count cards and how to know the first two cards that would be dealt. Beverly was a card shark/gambler/grifter/slight of hand artist extraordinaire, well enough known in the gambling industry that he was not allowed to play in any gambling establishment in Nevada. His illicit talents, however, made him a perfect and highly valued employee of any casino. While he wasn't allowed in any casino as a customer, Beverly could spot a fellow card-shark, dice-loader and dishonest in-house 21 or craps dealer a mile away, and he always had a job doing just that. Bev was an early and highly effective version of today's one way mirrors that sit in the ceilings above every table in every casino in Nevada so that players and dealers alike never know if they are being watched by the likes of Beverly Beverly. "Bev," as he was called, was balding and pale skinned and never went outdoors if he could help it. He was a casino creature and the first person I knew whose attention was complete. Bev was totally present, whether talking with my father, demonstrating his impressive array of card tricks to my parents' circle of friends, teaching me to shuffle and deal cards or standing in the pit watching the casino action for signs of his peers. Bev's gift was clarity and his presence like sunshine to me. The ultimate gamester and slight-of-hand artist, Bev was without agenda, judgment or deception in the company of friends, and I loved and trusted him for it. Whatever his reasons for being my friend, he alerted me to the significance of quality and qualities in a person, and I always felt respected, completely included, liked and, most important, safe in his presence.

In many ways my parents and other relatives and their friends (and enemies) were the pioneers of Lake Tahoe, more like the California pioneers of 100 years earlier than they realized or history has appreciated. Some, like Harvey and Llewellyn, would build an empire. Others, like mom and dad, would leave, moving on back to Reno from whence they began. Before that happened, I learned to love the mountains. To this day the sound of wind moving through pine trees has an effect on me like primal music heard in a great cathedral. During the summer months between Memorial Day and Labor Day the folks generally worked double shifts at Harvey's Wagon Wheel and, later, after Harvey and Dad had their fallout, at George's Gateway Casino. Dad was a superb craps and 21 dealer and he was a bookkeeper (more on that later) while Mom worked as a waitress, change girl and sometimes cook. (It was not until the 1950s that women were allowed to work in the better paying jobs of dealers in the gambling trade and that black entertainers like Sammy Davis Jr. and Louis Armstrong were allowed to work in Nevada's casinos as entertainers. Not until 1962 when Attorney General Robert Kennedy forced it upon them did the major Nevada casinos allow black people to enter the casinos as customers.) During the winters my folks collected unemployment and found part-time work for cash and somehow got by. Until I was in college my folks never owned a home and we lived in a succession of rentals, but we were never poor and always had plenty of food, clothing and, most important, free time for all those aspects of life not tied to American's economic machine which grinds up so many American lives. The freedom of my early life was a great gift including learning about self-determination, much of it involving long childhood rambles by myself in the mountains surrounding the sparsely populated Lake of the Sky, and, in winter, skiing.

Near our home in wintertime Zephyr Cove I kept a slalom hill packed out and in practice shape. For slalom poles I used willows, cut and stripped with a hand axe and sharpened at the thick end for easy insertion into snow. Most of the basic foundation of my knowledge of skiing and my relationship to that understanding was built on that slalom hill. It was solid, but like every underpinning the very scope of its construction determined what would and would not be built upon it. That is, I was largely a self-taught skier and I grew to love and rely upon solitary experience that was all my own, could not be taken from me, and was far removed if only for a few hours from the confusion and periodic waves of alcoholic sorrow that washed across my family. The outdoor experience, the learning and the process of side-stepping up and then skiing down my little slalom courses was refuge, classroom, path and sustenance. (More than 50 years later during a sad period I often went backcountry skiing alone in the mountains around Ketchum, Idaho where I live. A friend, a backcountry skier who is fearful of avalanche danger and injury and who would never go off the beaten path without a group of like-minded skiers, asked me why I skied alone where no immediate help is available in case of accident or disaster. "Therapy," I replied without thinking or hesitation.) The track of a ski in snow tells you a lot but not everything about the skiing that made it. As I hiked back up my hill after a run I studied my tracks which told me how close to the gate I had come. Even a beginner ski racer boy knew that being close to the gate was faster, but it took awhile to learn to read the more subtle aspects of track--line and arc of the turn, skid of the ski, angle of the edge--and their effect on time. I became a lone student of ski technique. On weekends at ski races and on the ski hill I watched and quizzed better skiers and talked with John Robinson and my other ski buddies about how to be faster, better and to win races. And I took it all back to my slalom hill for verification and refinement by reading my tracks in the snow, according to the evolving standards of my own skiing and understanding.

Within a year of putting on my first pair of skis I was Far West Ski Association four-event (downhill, slalom, jumping and cross-country) champion for the under 14 years set. Skiing changed and saved my life, giving me a place and space all my own to grow, learn and explore, different and independent from the world of my parents. I have written elsewhere: *"We were young ski racers in 1953, boys in love with an activity that took me out of myself into a world of mountains, snow, and crystal clean air and focused vision, out of the anger, confusion and encompassing fury of my particular set of circumstances within a rage-filled generation. Skiing, and, more specifically, ski racing probably saved my life, allowing me to grow into a social critic instead of the sociopath I might have become in response to society's violent and small-minded hypocrisies, pretensions and shallow smugness. Skiing kept anger, adolescent hormones and confusion in check enough to focus on a path that was to take me skiing all over the world. It formed and informed my life at least as much as the dynamics of family, the structure of schools, the warmth and generosity of true friends, the betrayals of false friends and the other (and normal) vicissitudes of life."*

The mountains and Lake Tahoe and skiing put me in daily touch with nature, the outdoors, physical activity and a clarity that touched my soul in ways that nothing else in life has, a perfect antidote, counter-point and yin to the yang of the society of my parents and their friends in the casino worlds of Tahoe after World War II.

Chapter V
EXITING PARADISE

"A mind not to be chang'd by place or time.
The mind is its own place, and in itself
Can make a heaven of hell, of hell a heaven."
John Milton

"Unless [artists] can remember what it was to be a little boy,
they are only half complete as artist and as man."
James Thurber

This is a memoir, based on a boy's observation and a man's memory. Observation is by the nature of the universe incomplete and memory by that same nature selective and distorted by time. A memoir is a collage of the new and the old, of the old better understood or at least understood in new ways, of understanding the new as being as old as the human heart and mind. The new is timeless and the eternal is always arriving anew.

We left Tahoe the first time in the fall of 1951. I was first and for me it was leaving paradise. For Mom and Dad it was the best of limited options. They tried to ease into the move by shipping me off to the Christian Brothers boy's school in Sacramento in order to instill some discipline, order and obedience into my being, which in their minds I needed. More importantly, the move would give them some breathing room from me to see what if anything could be done with their floundering relationship and the muddle they had made of their lives.

The layers and strands of family life are infinite and too complex for human understanding. At the heart (in the heart?) is the mystery, the inscrutable universe. At best, we can describe in words and understand with our own hearts and minds some of the heaven, a bit of the hell and the direction that leads home. At worst we deceive ourselves into believing we understand it and that our actions are guided by that understanding. It was nearly 35 years before I came to know by piecing together bits of memory and other shards of new information what exactly precipitated our move from Tahoe, my father's "falling out" with Uncle Harvey, our exit from Paradise. Roughly, it worked something like this: among other jobs he held with the Wagon Wheel, Dad was the bookkeeper, and he kept the books according to Harvey's instructions. That is, Harvey wasn't paying his full share of federal income tax and dad helped him mask that reality from the feds. Harvey was cheating on the feds and Dad was cheating on Harvey. Dad was skimming from the casino proceeds and Harvey either caught him at it or suspected him of it and fired him for it, and they never spoke again as long as they lived. Money is relative to need and desire, but even in Dad's concept of its use to him I don't think he stole major amounts. The closest I ever got him to define what happened was once when he said, "Well, I may have taken a twenty here and there." But it is the betrayal of trust among thieves that creates enemies between them, and this unfaithfulness on Father's part created a fracture line through an already fractious family that I certainly knew about and experienced on several levels but did not understand for many years. I didn't know and never would have thought that Father could be a thief or that he would be thoughtless and careless enough to get caught stealing from a relative who had so much power over our lives. Perhaps his resentment at being indebted to his wife's family for a favor was one reason he stole. I never knew him to be either greedy, addicted to anything that required money or particularly ambitious. Maybe he did it simply for the thrill.

Dad went to work for George's Gateway Club, Harvey's next door competitor, and Mom went with him to work as a change girl, sitting in a booth where gamblers could change their dollars into quarters and nickels and chips to be used at the tables and in the slot machines, and, when they won, changed back into dollars to take home. Within a year Dad got caught skimming from George as well, though it would take me years to put that together. It was Beverly Beverly who was working for George and caught Dad, and I was somehow present when Bev said to Dad without the slightest rancor or judgment, as only befitted such a card shark extraordinaire, "I couldn't believe my eyes when I saw what you were doing." Some thirty years would pass before I understood Bev's words and Dad's actions and why he suddenly wasn't working at George's Gateway any longer.

It was around then that I was shipped off to the Catholic boy's school for some discipline, shaping up and lessons in Christian morality and values. In retrospect it is clear that the folks were probably a bit desperate and must have sacrificed a great deal in order for me to attend what, as such things go, was probably a decent school, with no more dangers and warped ideas than are found in any other. But for me it was a disorienting cultural/social/emotional shock. In the space of one day I went from being an only child who had his own room and the rural community and mountains of the 1951 Tahoe Basin for a playground to a regimented Catholic boy's school (I had never been to church and had no religious training, preference or concepts) where I lived in a huge dorm room with more than 70 other boys in a vast, flat, hot, strange city called Sacramento. There was neither privacy nor freedom, and

I hated it from the first instant Mom and Dad dropped me off and drove away. From the perspective of adulthood, it is evident that I also resented being dumped out of my home into a generic environment for the second time in a life that hadn't even reached its teens. It may take an instant or a lifetime but resentment always reacts. This is as true for a people or a country as it is for an individual.

My reaction set a pattern for life.

Memories of the Brothers: Catechism. For a 12 year old boy without the slightest training, interest in or exposure to religious dogma, the Christian Brothers catechism class was extraordinarily bizarre. Perhaps it was the teachers or that catechism was obviously more important to the Brothers than English, history or recess. Because I hated being there I was honor bound (a child's sense of honor is strong, hidden as it may be from the world of adults) to resist that which was most important to those I instinctively opposed. Maybe I was simply fortunate enough to have my bullshit detector turned on at an early age without undue hardships and the cynicisms that grow from disappointments. My early training with Beverly Beverly gave me a solid foundation in the art of keeping your eye on the cards while not getting lost in the words of the dealer or his deals. Beverly Beverly was one of my first adult friends and I have always been grateful for the influence of his disreputable clarity and gambler's honesty about the human condition. Though I have since learned that catechism is touted to be a question and answer process, I remember that my questions for the most part were denigrated, shunted aside and never directly answered by any Christian Brother I encountered. I remember the fury of the response of one of the Brothers to my question, "Why do we have to memorize these poems?" I was told with anger drooling with disdain and disrespect that these texts to memorize were not poems, but, rather, sacred words to accept and live by and not question. This was not poetry. This was THE WORD. Who was I to question the holy word? Good question. I didn't have the answer, but I realized I was never going to find out from the Christian Brothers, each of whom would have been an easy read in a game of poker.

New friends. I was big for my age, a good looking even pretty boy who, for both obvious and less clear reasons was socially precocious and made friends easier with kids a couple of years older than with those my own age. I was in the 8th grade, considered junior high school, and I began to hang out during recesses with two boys from the 10th grade, which was high school. The Brothers considered this inappropriate social interaction, and I was told that my two new friends were "too old" for me to hang with, and whenever they would see us together the Brothers would separate us and we would all be reprimanded. After a couple of reprimands my two friends avoided me, and I perceived myself as without friends or even allies in a hostile environment. Of course I might have made other friends, found allies in an unsympathetic world, persevered and made the best of a situation every instinct in my being told me was destructive and corruptive of my best interests. There are thousands and thousands of fine human beings, productive members of society, assets to humanity and their communities who have survived and even benefited from a Christian Brothers education, and I commend and recognize them. But it was not for me and I commend and recognize my instincts for letting me know that when I wasn't old enough to tell the difference between my God given instincts and the man made Ten Commandments. I was homesick for the mountains and the freedoms of an only child's life of roaming the woods of the Tahoe basin as much as I was for Mom and Dad. After I couldn't hang with my two new friends I was friendless at

Christian Brothers, and in retrospect it seems I kept it that way for good reason.

Two Brothers. There were two Brothers whose names I've forgotten who seemed to be in charge of my dorm. I know Christian Brothers wear black robes, but my memory is that they dressed in brown. To a boy used to his own solitary amusements they were a constant omnipresence on the playground, in the dorm, everywhere. It was these two who forbade me having friends a couple of years older. In response, I separated myself from the other boys in my dorm and class and so I was, in turn, easily separated, and the two Brothers several times called me into a room where it was just me and the two of them. They questioned me about my attitude and whether I was happy and talked to me in a manner I did not like at all. They were not so much threatening as obsequiously menacing. They were "nice," but they gave me the creeps. While Beverly Beverly was a card shark con-man, a street-smart hustler who could not be trusted with a deck of cards in any casino, he was honest, trustworthy and my friend. My instincts told me he would never hurt me and would protect me against anyone who might. Those same instincts told me that the two Brothers were dangerous to my well being and were to be avoided at any cost and every opportunity. Praise the Lord for an intact, well-functioning nervous system that indicated in the language of nature that precedes speech that whatever the Brothers represented was not for me. I'd take the wisdom of the cards over that of the robes. Fifty years later, I was an adult contemplating the significance of the distasteful spectacle of the Catholic Church's ethical/moral/dogmatic/economic/ contortionist gymnastics on behalf of protecting and hiding its pedophilic priests and impenetrable institution at the expense of the children within them before the obvious struck me of how lucky I had been as a 12 year old to stay one step and instinct ahead of those Christian Brothers buggers.

The escape. Blessed are those who act upon instinct immediately. One sunny Sacramento afternoon about six weeks into my Christian Brothers education I took my life savings (about $30 in small bills and change hidden in a sock in the bottom of my suitcase) and left the school and walked downtown to a movie theatre. I phoned my parents at Tahoe and announced I'd run away. I reached them before the Brothers discovered I was missing. Needless to say, they were not pleased. Dad was particularly disturbed and grew angry and threatening and loud over the phone and insisted I return immediately to the school. I hung up without reply and went to a movie and ate a bag of popcorn. The film was "Edward, My son," with Spencer Tracy, a downer movie if there ever was one, particularly for a 13 year old boy in my situation. Most of the film was over my head. The popcorn was good. I relished being in a dark place where no one could find me. It pleased and amused me that my parents could not reach, find, threaten, control, manipulate or even communicate with me. When the film was over and the popcorn gone I again phoned Mom and Dad, who had by then been notified by the Brothers that I was missing. They wanted to know exactly where I was, but I wasn't telling. My father made one last threat that eventually they would find me and when they did they were taking me back to the school. I insisted that wasn't going to happen. It went back and forth like this for awhile and the longer it went on the more I felt what modern pop psychology refers to as "empowered." I knew I'd won the battle if not the war when I told Dad that even if he found me and took me back to the Brothers I would only run away again, and next time I wouldn't phone him. I meant it and he knew I meant it and I knew he knew. Dad and I, like most fathers and sons, had our ups and downs and disagreements and misunderstandings and conflicts, but we had a fortunate ability to get very clear about some of the important issues of life. In that ability is the taproot of good and lasting friendship, and it enabled us to continue to grow our friendship through some difficult times until his death nearly 50 years later.

The immediate solution was for me to phone Uncle Jim Barkley, my mother's brother, who lived in Sacramento and had already been notified that I was loose somewhere in town. His daughter, Barbara, one of my favorite older cousins, came to get me and we went back to Jim's where I was treated like visiting royalty. Jim and his family were loving, kind, generous people for whom family was the core of their lives, and in retrospect it is clear they realized that something besides willful stubbornness had initiated my escape from the Brothers. I've always loved them for their generosity on that occasion and cherished and remembered the sense of relief I felt in their home.

It didn't last long.

A day or two later Mom and Dad came to pick me up. Mom was quiet and passive, subdued, probably embarrassed in front of her brother by a son so disobedient and different from her brother's children. Dad, on the other hand, was as close to rage as I'd ever seen him. Usually when he was angry it was German/Dutch cold and calculating; but this was close to that German/Dutch far side of him that might lose control, the side that got drunk and beat until it broke a child's drum at Christmas, an aspect of his personality that he kept locked down most of the time. Perhaps he would have lived a life more rich and full and satisfying if he had let it out, let loose, damned the consequences and been himself more often. Or maybe he knew or intuited that letting it out might have destroyed the world. They picked me up at Uncle Jim's, pausing only a few minutes to visit with relatives seldom seen, and we drove to the Christian Brothers School to retrieve my things.

The Brothers were very polite and tried to be friendly and talk with me in a kind manner. I'm sure they were relieved that I was okay and hadn't gotten myself into some awful trouble. They told me I was welcome to stay and try again and there were no recriminations from them. But I was determined and got my things and got in the car with Mom and Dad. Mom didn't say much, but Dad verbally flayed me. I don't remember exactly what he said, but whatever it was it caused me to cry. I remember that. And I remember that when I started to cry he castigated me even more for crying and told me that I was a "sissy" for "crying like a little girl." I remember those things and feeling bad and lonely and desolate. It was a day that cut deep and nearly 15 years would pass before another tear passed from my eye.

It seems to me now that sending me to the Catholic school was a step in my parents' attempt to break up their impossible marriage and find a way to get on with their lives without the millstone of their son and without mistreating that son. Any plans or intentions they imagined were sabotaged when I left Christian Brothers. At first we moved back to Clayton where Dad worked in a Pittsburgh steel factory and Mom opened a small coffee shop and I went to school. They lived in a trailer and I lived in a tent next to the trailer. I rode my bike, played football at school, made a few friends and went to weekend matinees at the theatre in Concord where I necked in the back row with Carmadean and caressed and kissed my first female breast with wonder and affection and unbelievable desire. Except for skiing, that was the coolest, most enjoyable and intriguing thing I'd ever discovered. For better or worse, the wonders of woman and the adventure of skiing would define and guide much of my subsequent life.

The primary benefits I gained from the Christian Brothers were an abiding distrust of authority, a fine tuning of my God given shit-detector, a deep faith in the supreme truth of my own instincts and the knowledge that religious devotees were no brighter, wise, well intentioned or better people than card sharks and misguided parents. My brief schooling with the Christian Brothers gave me invaluable tools for building a life and understanding its processes. It was a fine education and I am grateful for it and to the Brothers for the teaching and to my parents for instigating it.

Chapter VI
THE WINTER OF 1952

"Mais ou sont les neiges d'antan?"
Francois Villon

*"In the depth of winter, I finally discovered that within me
there lay an invincible summer."*
Albert Camus

*"The Eskimo has fifty-two names for snow because it is
important to them; there ought to be as many for love."*
Margaret Atwood

I was 13 years old when we came back to live near
Stateline on the South Shore of Tahoe where the imaginary
border dividing California and Nevada makes its southern exit
from the deep blue of those most beautiful of unparted waters,
before slashing across the Sierra into the eastern desert along a
path recognized in all nature only in the mind of man. Our
home that winter was a small two-story house just behind the
Quonset hut Lakeside Theatre which was as crucial, formative
and important to my young life as school and home itself. In
that time of America the movie house and the art form shown
within was the home of the emotional and intellectual life of
young people. The experience of sitting in a movie house
eating popcorn and holding hands was erotic, mysterious,
inspiring and demanded one's full attention. A night at the
movies was more adventure than mindless entertainment. I
worked as a projectionist at the Lakeside that winter, a good
job within the capabilities and interests of an adolescent who

had school, skiing and the great Sierra Nevada winter to occupy daytime energies. The job assured me of Hollywood spellbound nights at every new film. To pre-television small mountain communities like Tahoe in those long gone days before it devolved into a tinsel Mecca for sybarites, a night at the movies was among the primary social, cultural and poetic events, especially for kids. Movies and radio provided mountain people their chief sources of information about the larger world.

Every small town in America had a movie house showing its own last picture show. It is unimaginable to have been an American youth in the 1950s without Hollywood's cornball romances and epic adventures and the celluloid courage epitomized by cowboys and soldiers under fire. Bravery is easy on film when danger is edited in, every normal fear conquered or edited out and death and maiming are not quite real. In later years I wondered how many young and old boys were blown away, blown apart, blown up in Vietnam and, at this writing, Iraq because their heads were full of fantastical celluloid and, later, televised and digitalized images of actor soldiers miraculously dodging and shooting bullets that somehow lacked the punch and consequences they have in real life. "C'mon, men," they said on screen, "let's move out and get them Gooks." In real life they said, "Aw, shit, the flesh is real," and died.

My bedroom was upstairs in that old house. A door from my room opened to an elevated sun deck over the kitchen. During part of that extraordinary winter we had to dig down through the snow to the sun deck door to gain entrance to the house. At 13 I viewed the huge snowfalls and inconvenience as magic and great adventure to be cherished and enjoyed. The trade off was the loss of privacy in my treasured sanctuary/bedroom as my secret escape/entrance hatch to the outside world became the front and only door to the family home.

The winter of 1952 still exists in words spoken and written and in the brain cells and living tissue of experience among those who lived then in the Sierra. Its continuing presence is marked in the geology and along river and stream banks and in the growth rings of trees in the forests and secured among the many guardians of the history of the land. The City of San Francisco, America's most luxurious passenger train was stopped by snow at Yuba Gap near Donner Summit. Passengers and crew were dressed and prepared for the weather in Chicago or San Francisco, not for 30 foot snow drifts on the side of a steep hill near the wind swept crest of the Sierra Nevada in the decade's biggest snowstorm. As travelers tend to do (and we are all travelers), they had not considered every possibility on the road between commencement and destination of the journey. If every potential of the journey were examined for consequences humanity would have perished long before history came along to record its many follies and adventures. That winter those people huddled in wool blankets in dark, cold train cars, nibbling at rationed but sufficient food supplies. Human nature being the biology based cornucopia of laughter and tears and joy and travail that it is, those storm bound travelers undoubtedly have some earthy tales and memories of their Sierra snowstorm, some obtainable only in the private souls of those who lived them or in the karmic records that all write and few read.

Thousands of deer, elk, moose and other wild creatures died of starvation and exhaustion as their normally lean winter food supply was inaccessibly buried across the west. Sharp hoofed beasts wore themselves to exhaustion plowing and sinking through unending snow until there was no place left except death. It was a disaster for western livestock, though the livestock industry alleviated it somewhat by air drops of food to snowbound bovines. The airlift didn't entirely leave out wildlife, and many desperate ungulates up to their bellies in snow must have gone through a bizarre progression from the weakness of starvation despair in the face of the final option to helpless terror at the sound and sight of throttled down multi-engine transport planes making low passes above them to wonder, amazement and perhaps a sense of mystic intervention from ungulate heaven as bales of food dropped from the sky like nourishing meteorites--inescapably taking out a few with direct hits instead of saving them as intended--to the gratefulness of food in an empty stomach, to the freedom of life and the chance to survive until the next hunting season.

The roads to Stateline were closed, power lines were down and only owners of battery powered radios could huddle around the fireplace listening to news reports of the outside world doing battle with the storm. My family was fortunate. Within a mile of our house were a couple hundred other souls, a grocery called Cecil's Market, a doctor, and Stateline's casinos and saloons to salve the parents' claustrophobic need for alcohol fueled socializing. We had a large, black with gold lettering, short-wave, battery driven Zenith radio. By the time the storm ended and roads opened Cecil's had been stripped of everything fresh and edible and most things canned, bottled or packaged. Via the marvelous Zenith we seldom missed a news report, George Burns and Gracie Allen, Jack Benny, The Shadow, the Lone Ranger and nearly any kind of music I could find, especially late at night in my room alone when the magic of music allowed my imagination to roam in worlds not easily found at snowbound Lake Tahoe.

We were fortunate but we were trapped, and a covert panic was discernable even to a 13 year old. Those few with mountaineering experience could have skied or snow shoed over Kingsbury Grade to Genoa in the Carson Valley where commerce still moved, food was available, isolation alleviated. Most people were unprepared to move as much as a mile through snow without the aid of some form of the internal combustion engine. Mom would certainly have perished of cold and fear and ignorance of what to do if she had been forced to get out of the Tahoe Basin on her own. It would have been tight for Dad either way. My family's survival and mobility was typical of the larger society on which it depended. I remember my folks and their friends joking about the Donner Party, that unfortunate group of westward travelers caught out by the epic, early Sierra winter of 1846-47, the granddaddy myth of Sierra wintertime against which every Sierra snowstorm is measured at some substratum of men's minds. The Donner Party was a group of men, women and children trying to get to California in covered wagons. They made a couple of mistakes and got trapped by early snow near what is now known as Donner Lake at the east foot of Donner Pass. When California gained statehood three years later Donner Lake was nearly 20 miles within its imaginary border. The Donner Party had in fact made it to California, but not over the Sierra Nevada to the mild, temperate parts they had in mind. Eighty two were caught out by November snows in two camps, one near present Truckee, the other on the east end of Donner Lake. After the grimmest winter any of them would ever know, 47 made it out in April to the western lowlands of the California of their dreams and a totally different significance and importance. Those who survived did so by breaking civilization's taboo on cannibalism, gnawing the sustenance of life from the wasted, lean flesh of dead mates, relatives and friends who proved too weak or unlucky for the situation. The Donner Party has come to have a significance recognized far beyond the Sierra, a story of tragedy, poor judgment, bad luck, taboos broken, courage, endurance, faith, survival, compassion, cold hearts, great generosity and a common empathy glowing across the years in the souls of people contemplating the circumstances and consequences of being snowbound and cut off from the normal currents of human society. Adlai Stevenson, a great American largely unrecognized, said, "A hungry man is not a free man." And men without freedom are damaged and damned and sometimes destroyed by any course of action open to them. Whether the oppressor is a snowstorm, a dictator, weapon in the hand of a soldier/child, neurosis, addiction or a war there is no way out that avoids pain, loss, sorrow, permanent scars and restriction in those fortunate enough to break free. Only the survivors of the Donner Party can decide if they were fortunate or cursed, but their dilemma periodically confronts some pocket of humanity trapped by fate in an isolated disaster, cut off from the larger society and the sustaining gifts of a provident earth, reduced as humans in undreamed of ways. Stateline is less than 40 air miles from Donner Lake, and the Donner Party story was well known to Tahoe citizens in 1952. All humor is truth betrayed or, perhaps, only revealed, and there were some dark, earthy, tasteless (sic) remarks in the nervous humor of my parents' social circle that winter. Some of these jokesters must have thought over their moral and practical choices and priorities when options are reduced to starvation or dining on a neighbor, friend, mate or blood relative. That blood is thicker than water is a two way street, hey?

A few days before the roads to Stateline succumbed to the snows I came down with a cold. A retired doctor lived nearby. He was a shaking old man who supplemented his retirement by providing limited medical service to a doctorless citizenry. The old guy gave me a shot of penicillin in the buttock for treatment of my cold. Penicillin, the miracle drug, slayer of gangrene, gonorrhea, mild infections and the common cold has proved not to be the marvel it once seemed, though it has an assured place in the pharmacological spectrum. Penicillin has saved millions of lives and unimaginable human misery, but I am strongly allergic to its powers. First arrived the hives, great welts the size of bull frogs on my head and arms and back and legs. They disfigured and itched and were a nuisance, but I felt okay and it was decided by minds distrustful of pleasure and the senses that I had been eating too many sweets, a premise that might have been true but which would not have fit the consequences. Two days later my entire body began to swell: hands, feet, arms and legs doubled in size within a few hours. My extremities looked like huge sausages in human skin. Pain prevented me from standing. I was confined to bed and could not eat, defecate, urinate nor sleep. I sweated. Right then the roads closed. Mom and Dad turned some frantic as the biggest storm in recent history settled over the Sierra. I was a very sick and terribly uncomfortable boy in bed, neither frantic nor particularly cognizant. The old doctor came by and observed that I was probably allergic to penicillin, that it was a dangerous situation for me, and that nothing could be done until the roads opened. I sweated and pained and endured and nibbled on some white Wonder bread toast covered in butter, sugar and cinnamon and drank some tea to replace the liquid sweat. Mom and Dad took turns at the side of my bed waiting on me and I was never alone when that made all the difference. Now that I am a man and have sat at night with my own sick child, I appreciate how frightened and powerless my parents felt as their son's body swelled grotesquely while the snow continued to fall and isolation grew in their minds.

Like so many crises my sickness and swelling eventually subsided, as did the storm. I escaped unscathed this time, though I would be told that the next shot of penicillin would probably kill me. Along with other Sierra Nevada residents of the time and mountain people of every age and place, my family survived through enforced patient endurance.

Though it was not the end of that winter, the opening of the road to Stateline from Carson City, 30 miles away, was a memorable event. The word spread: "The plows are coming; the plows are coming." Everybody who was able gathered at Stateline to watch them plow the last mile. In the lead was a big orange double blade V snowplow furrowing through the deep snow. Staggered closely behind were two also orange snow blowers, one on either side of the plow's path, widening the cut and shooting giant sprays of snow high in the air along the newly created artery to the world. We had been snowbound for two weeks, and the road opening was a grand and thrilling sight.

When the plows reached Stateline a grateful populace took the crews into Uncle Harvey's saloon for a necessary and heartily felt celebration that lasted well into the next day, a fest that became part of local legend. Neither the crews nor many locals made it home that night, but we had made it through another Sierra snowstorm.

The creation is ultimately mysterious and powerful with concerns beyond those of man. Within that mystery hides the purpose and path of mankind. A bit of it unfolds in every Sierra snowstorm. Humans tend to view things through the exclusive and limited field of vision of a human life. Our normal daily thoughts are not large enough for contemplating the slow formation and dissolution of glaciers and the sculpting and wearing down of mountain ranges. We see first in Sierra snowstorms what interferes with or facilitates our personal interest in getting home on time, having powder snow to ski in the morning, shoveling roof or walkway, summer water for farming and sustaining flatland cities, getting over Donner Pass or through the night without freezing or dining on your neighbor or dying of starvation. That is how we should and must see things, carefully and in cautious detail, for we are small and time bound creatures with enormous power and significance in our every thought and action. Our lives come and are here for a time and then vanish like Sierra snowstorms, some big and memorable, others small and soon forgotten, each leaving its mark and forever altering the world with its individual crystal of unique, precious beauty that all too soon melts into common water and flows back home to the sea.

END BOOK ONE

BOOK TWO

Chapter I
HIGH SCHOOL IN THE BIGGEST LITTLE
CITY IN THE WORLD

"The best throw of dice is to throw them away."
English Proverb

*"It is, indeed, one of the capital tragedies of youth--and youth
is the time of real tragedy--that the young are thrown mainly
with adults they do not quite respect."*
H.L. Mencken

On the first day of high school in the fall of 1952 Father drove me across town to the new brick structure that was Reno High School in the family car, a gray 1941 Plymouth coupe with gear shift on the steering column. Father had taught me the rudiments of driving a couple of years before and sat in the passenger seat while I guided the machine around and around the one loop road of our Zephyr Cove neighborhood on the east shore of Lake Tahoe where we lived before my exile to the Christian Brothers. He didn't ask me how I felt about the day or the strange new school with more than a hundred times more kids my age than the school at Tahoe. Instead, he spoke of the dangers and rules and mechanics of driving a car in a city. It was more complicated and perilous than driving in the mountains, he said. He must have thought my sullen inattention was due to adolescent hormones and anxiety about starting a new school year at a new school in a new town. This was partly true, but boredom and resentment gusted through my being like the winds that came off the east side of the Sierra and through Washoe Valley and Reno and across the great Nevada high desert and mountain landscape.

Boredom, among children as well as adults, is more laziness, failure to pay attention to the moment at hand and fear of personal inadequacy than any lack on the part of the universe to provide. The bored human is less alive than the dumbest chicken, cow, spider, ant or crow, none of which are ever bored. Boredom is a narcotic, more addictive, damaging and prevalent than heroin or even alcohol and less enjoyable than either. Besides, boredom is.....boring.

Resentment is a stage of American adolescence, a phase some take into adulthood and some into death. There is so very much to resent in this life if resentment is the attitude of choice, and, at the age of 13, I resented the adult world's obvious and myriad imperfections which I was required to cope with and was powerless to rectify. No wonder I was resentful. Any group of people as incompetent and unhappy as my parents and many of their friends (and relatives) and who finally took me to Paradise in the Tahoe Basin and then tore me away to live in Reno--Reno!!!!--was clearly not to be respected and deserved my resentment.

Besides, Dad was giving me driving lessons in a car I had already stolen several times and taken on 85 mph midnight spins and had proven to myself that at the wheel I was as invincible as he was cautious. And just a few weeks before we moved to Reno I managed to steal the old Plymouth (where almost two years earlier while it was parked in the Wagon Wheel Saloon parking lot Joanne Faye, who had apple red lips and nice tits she would never let me touch, had given me my first passionate kiss and serious make out session) and made it to the Drive In Movie with a girl whose name I don't remember but I managed to fondle, kiss, suck, lick and adore her warm, bulbous boobs with hard nipples that could put your eye out if you weren't careful. My heart might have failed or exploded with ecstasy and joy or, since that's all she would let me fondle, irreconcilable frustration if my heart hadn't been so young and healthy and strong. I knew a lot more about how to drive that car than Dad suspected and I had had a great deal more fun in it than he was having. He didn't seem to notice that cars were made for fun.

No wonder I was filled with boredom and resentment.

Dad drove into the huge asphalt parking lot by the one year old red brick rectangle that accommodated more than 2000 students, including its first freshman class of which I was a member. I got out. "Phone me if you need a ride home," he said, and drove away.

Fear. Confusion. Though I'd been born in Reno and had lived there as a child (I was a big boy now), Tahoe was the home of my heart, experience and friends. Two days earlier we had moved into the basement of a friend's home at 134 West Pueblo Street, less than a block from the home of the girl who would become my first wife less than seven years later. I stood alone in the parking lot in the presence of more people my own age than I'd ever seen in one place. I searched in vain for one of the four or five Reno people I knew through ski racing. It was a new experience and I was terrified. With my heart in my throat and not on my sleeve I entered the crowded, sterile, tiled halls of Reno High with its right angles and straight lines and rows of identical lockers between doors leading into mostly identical classrooms. O, what had become of my life among the mountain meadows, streams and the ever-changing perfect blue waters of Lake Tahoe with lullaby mountain winds in the pine trees at night? I immediately felt that I was an alien spirit caught behind enemy lines in the hostile land of the institution.

Intuition said I was in for a lengthy guerrilla fight and to be ready for it. Intuition and heart are among one's finest friends and are to be trusted, and I did.

An orientation lecture to the freshman class in the gymnasium set the tone. The school principal, David Finch, began by pointing out the difference in meaning and spelling between 'principle' and 'principal.' A principle was a code of conduct by which a person lived. A principal was your 'pal' who would help you to live by proper principles. Finch seemed more mechanical than spontaneous to me, his chuckle at his own humor more studied than heartfelt. For the four years I attended Reno High School I never saw anything to allow me to change my initial impression of Finch as a prissy, priggish, cold, tight ass who viewed himself and everyone else in the school as parts in a well-run machine. The whole was more important than any or all of its parts, a concept with an obvious simplicity and beauty that has been wholeheartedly embraced by nations, states, institutions, tribes, teams, corporations, armies, religions, dictators, tyrants and movements throughout man's tumultuous history. The flaw in such simplification of nature's complexities is that when each part is not as important as the whole the parts come undone and, eventually, so does the whole. The first thing to be decided, he told us, was which subjects to pursue. The guidelines we should use in choosing courses of study that would occupy our time and energies and human potential for the next four years depended on what kind of student we would be. There were only two kinds: those who would continue on to college, and those who would not.

Finch rightfully emphasized academic achievement. He pointed out that those who don't continue on to college were no lesser people than those of more ambition and mental capacity and higher goals; but he told us to consider carefully what it means to be prepared for the....ahhhhhh.....'lesser skilled' jobs in our society. And then he added with a chuckle that somebody had to do them. If we weren't going to college, he said, we should pursue such classes as auto-mechanics, wood shop, drafting, short-hand and typing, all good ways to learn skills using the hands rather than the brain. Those students planning on attending college should study math, science, English, history and languages. From the very first day of school even the principal, our pal, divided students along pre-determined lines. Something about it (and Finch) pissed me off from the beginning. He wasn't deceptive or wrong in his advice, and from his perspective he was well intentioned. Nevertheless, there was an underlying message that I did not like and have never accepted. Perhaps it was more the way he presented it and the hidden assumptions about people he implied that caught my attention. Maybe the time with the Christian Brothers had helped me be more mindful of the subtleties of what authority said and wanted one to do. I was 13 and already wary of authority itself. The Christian Brothers had inadvertently given me the foundation of the best education a young American boy of the early 1950s could have. The Brothers did and do pride themselves on being superior teachers, apparently giving themselves a pass around the perils of pride, but I never learned to trust Finch as I had learned to flee the Brothers, and the similarities of manipulation and smug insincerity toward their students were clear to me.

Beware of smugness, particularly when authoritative and self-righteous. Fifteen years later "Question Authority" was a mantra as well as a staple of basic intelligence and an indispensable tool of survival in America. In all systems, including educational, the system itself eventually supersedes the purpose of the system in the hearts and minds of those who live within and from that system. They are necessary and can be beneficial and dependable, but systems are not infallible and easily lead to replacing thought with habit, purpose with power. Habitual thought or action are life's enemies. To question is not an indication of disrespect, as respect or lack thereof can only grow from the answer to the question.

Still, I didn't want to be a dummy or grow into a man of lesser skills, and I followed Finch's advice and signed up for college prep courses. I was a mediocre student at best, and on clear winter days in classrooms on the south side of the building in sight of the beautiful snow covered Sierra I listened to lectures with half or less a mind while drawing slalom courses in my notebooks and penciling in various lines through the gates until I found one that seemed best. I did well in subjects I fancied and got by in those I didn't. I struggled with all my studies and with the Reno High School administration every winter because ski racing took me away from school for long periods of time. While I was bright enough and eager to learn, ski racing was more important to me than school. I wanted the system to meet my needs as a student who wanted to ski race, and the system did not, and, to be fair, could not, accommodate skiing the way it did football, basketball, track and baseball.

High school was a struggle. From the beginning I was at odds with significant members of both the administration and my fellow students. It wasn't something I set out to do or wanted. Nobody wants to be disliked or marginalized, but it was clearly my own doing. By the tender age of 13 I had learned to disdain conformity, question authority, distrust the majority of adults as a separate species, and, most tellingly, determine that none of the role models available to me would do. I eventually found a group of friends, all of them one to three classes and years ahead of me, and a few good teachers I liked, respected and trusted. I was never able to swim in the mainstream, though I tried a few times. Freshman hazing by the senior class the first week of school set the tone. Freshman boys at RHS were required to wear ties outside the collar, put shirts on backwards, wear different color socks and roll pants up to the knees for an entire week. Though harmless fun to some, that seemed demeaning nonsense to me and I didn't do it. Perhaps I had been corrupted by those Tahoe years when I learned to amuse myself with only the beautiful lake, the surrounding mountains, trees, rocks, caves and meadows as secretive, benevolent spirits for companions. I already missed solitary swims and hikes and sitting on the deserted Zephyr Cove beach watching sun abandon sky and disappear behind the western Sierra Nevada across the purest of blue water lakes in that time before progress, population, pollution, freeways and man's greed so carelessly scarred its beauty and eutrophicated its waters. Perhaps it was those years of books in the night before the fireplace, chess and cribbage with Father, making candy with Mother, skiing in the backyard alone until dark, and a lot of early age independence and, in truth, solitude with its resultant appreciation of those people who came my way with respect that made it repugnant and impossible to put a shirt on backwards and wear different colored socks and roll my pant legs up to the knees and otherwise play the fool to a tradition my instincts and eyes (and, in truth, uptight fear and distrust) told me was corrupt and not in my best interests. There may have been other reasons but RHS was never a comfortable or entirely happy fit for me and vice-versa. The first day I came to school in normal attire was not too bad. The Senior Patrol which policed such matters told me to be in costume the next day. The morning after that was immediately harder as it was obvious I hadn't just forgotten. That knowledge engendered ugliness in some members of the patrol who cornered me in the school hall. The patrol that year was composed mostly of members of the football team (State champions that year and one of the best in Nevada history). The leader was Dick Bankofier, a 180 pound right end, the most intelligent of the bunch who I later came to like; but to me at that moment he was only a cocksure bully who meant harm. Years later I was saddened when a careless buck-fevered hunter mistook Dick for a deer and shot and killed him in the dark as he sat on a horse beside his 16 year old son waiting for the opening of hunting season in the hills above Reno. But when I was 13 and he and his friends had me cornered, threatened and afraid in the halls of RHS I would have shot him myself and not by mistake had I the opportunity. Don Manoukian, a clever minded 5 foot 6 inch 240 pound guard who had to shave twice a day was also on the patrol. Needless to explain, Don had a certain influence upon his peers and later in the day saved me a sound thrashing from a less benevolent senior. Don went on to be an All-American and professional football player and then a professional wrestler of considerable repute. With them was Hank DiRicco, a fine athlete in several sports who was big and strong and reeked of malevolence toward me with the perpetual frown of the scowler. He seemed particularly enraged with me and kept calling me an "ass-hole," "shit-head," and "a little turd." He said he would "knock the crap" out of me if I weren't in costume by lunchtime when he was personally going to make life shitty for me. Recognizing anal neuroses was beyond my scope at 13, but I was properly alarmed by a 190 pound deranged fullback on a crusade against my person and backed by his senior patrol peers.

I told them to leave me alone and hurried off to my next class under the combined protection of several hundred school mates and teachers whose sense of propriety did not permit beatings and mayhem in the hallways. These self-righteous bullies would not be dissuaded and at lunch time eight of them found me, picked me up, carried me to a car in the parking lot and we drove to Idlewild Park, next to Reno High. They called me a number of unpleasant names and I said nothing, though I was filled with an adolescent mixture of rage, fear, disbelief and disrespect. We piled out on the grass next to the duck/geese pond and Bankofier told me I had my last chance. I was outnumbered 8 to 1 and outweighed at least 10 to 1, and all I had to do was roll up my pant legs and wear a tie the next day and nothing would happen. But all I said was "No, leave me alone."

That shocked them. They had called my bluff and I'd returned the favor. There was a pause pregnant with possibilities ranging from me getting away with it and them leaving me alone to death to expulsion from school to tortures too gruesome to imagine to an old-fashioned ass-kicking. Mine. DiRicco broke the silence. "You little shit," he said, moving toward me with menace and what seemed to me imminent violence. If I could have made a run for it I would have, but I had seniors on three sides and the pond on the other. Accordingly I backed up to the edge of the pond and got ready to plant one foot as hard as I could kick into Hank's groin before he tore my head off and ate it, blood and brains dripping out the corners of his sneer, my blood and brains.

Manoukian stepped in. "Don't hurt him," he said in a matter of fact way that truly carried weight.

"Let's just throw him in the pond," Bankofier said.

"Don't hurt him," Manoukian reiterated.

"Leave me alone," I said.

"You're going in the drink, you little shit," DiRicco snarled, and he was right.

They rushed with the technique and power of the best high school football team in Nevada and grabbed me--DiRicco, Bankofier, Manoukian, Frank Keever and others who just stood around--before I could take a swing or place a kick and with a one-two-three swinging cadence they lofted me as far out into the Idyllwild duck pond as they could throw. I relaxed in the air not out of defeat or default but rather out of the instinctive knowledge that you can get hurt as easily and badly by fighting against whatever flight you are taking and its inevitable landing as you can by allowing others to determine who you are and who you will be. I lofted through the warm autumn Reno air and landed with a splash in a filthy, stagnant pond rife with ducks and geese and their shit and who knows what else. I was pissed. It's a good thing I didn't have a pistol handy when I hit that vile water because I would have, at least so I fantasized, surely and gladly shot as many members of the senior patrol as possible. Instead, unarmed and harmless, I stood up in the foul, brown, waist deep water, my shoes sunk in unspeakable mud and slime, and hand splashed as many of the senior patrol as weren't quick enough to get out of the way. That was all I could do, so I did it, the most natural action/re-action there can be. Do what you can do.

The entire bunch hurried out of splash range with the agility of high school athletic champions. They looked back at me. We regarded each other by a distance that had just increased by several light years. My hatred for those pricks was so complete that there was nothing for it to do but dissolve. That couldn't happen for awhile, but they laughed as if they'd just won a football game and climbed back into their cars and drove away, leaving me alone in the slime duck pond of Idyllwild Park. These were the leaders of RHS citizenry and it was clear that I needed to seek my life training elsewhere. Survival for me was not to be found in the direction of whatever the senior patrol had to teach.

I climbed out of the water and walked an hour across town to the basement of the tiny house on West Pueblo Street. I was humiliated, furious and uncomfortable, though nearly dried out by the time I got home. Mom just said, "Well, what did you expect to happen?" Dad told me to do what I thought was right but to be careful. My parents maintained the healthy practice of not interfering with life's lessons as they came for their son unless absolutely necessary or requested. I appreciated that then, and appreciate it even more now.

The next day I returned to school dressed in normal attire. I don't remember how my classmates related to me, but since I didn't yet know any of them I probably ignored them for the most part. I was called out of one of the morning's first classes for a meeting in the vice-principal's office. Andrew Rosaschi, the RHS VP, was a man I would encounter often. A note was brought to my classroom by a member of the hall patrol. My teacher interrupted the class to write me a hall pass. Everyone had heard about the events of the day before and all eyes watched as I left the room. I didn't hurry through the tiled, characterless hall. I took in deep breaths and let them out slowly, something an old ski jumper, Chet Zoberski, had taught me was a good thing to remember whenever you're scared or nervous. Take it in deep, let it out slow. A mantra for life. Rosaschi's secretary was expecting me and let me into his office and he told me to sit down in a chair facing him across his desk. We sized each other up. I have no idea what he saw or thought of a 13 year old boy who looked him in the eye while taking deep breaths, but I saw a man who, like Finch, had impeccable posture and dress, each strand of his pomaded dark hair in place. He wore rimless glasses perched atop a long, skinny nose sticking out from a lean face criss-crossed with red veins. In later years I would come to think of and refer to men like the vice-principal as "suits," mid-level bureaucrats in a system that encouraged, rewarded, insisted on and produced people who exemplify Winston Churchill's chilling summation of the German character, "Either at your feet or at your throat."

"It's been brought to my attention that you were absent from all your afternoon classes yesterday," he said, peering at me from cold eyes.

"Yes, that's right," I replied, taking deep breaths, letting them out slowly, slowly.

"Well-l-l-l-l-llllllll," he intoned with a backward tilt of his head as if regarding a suspicious troll peering out at him from under a dark bridge, "you aren't allowed to just leave school whenever you wish. We have rules about attending classes and we give demerits for missing them. Unless, of course," and he leaned across his desk toward me as if we were sharing a secret and I leaned in my chair away from him, "you had a good reason for your absence. In that case we might be able to excuse you without any demerits."

Breathe deep. Let it out slowly. Whatever he was up to set off every red flag/alarm bell in my young being. I didn't know what a demerit was (it turned out to be a sort of brownie point system of measuring student good citizenship, or, viewed another way, a Pavlovian form of student control), but within 30 seconds of meeting him Rosaschi felt like a threat. He looked and felt malicious and I did not trust him at all and when I left RHS four years later my sense of him had not changed one scintilla.

"Now, tell me," he continued, with a trace of a smile on his tightly controlled face, "what caused you to miss your afternoon classes yesterday."

He knew! He knew! I knew he knew! But one minute with him made my dislike and fear of the Senior Patrol seem like minor annoyances. The senior bullies might throw me in a filthy pond, beat me to a pulp, tear off my head and have it for lunch, but Rosaschi had bigger fish to fry, so to speak. My every instinct told me unequivocally that the VP could and would damage me far worse and in far more lasting ways than the seniors ever could, or would. The patrol might be my obstacle, but he was my enemy.

"I fell in the pond at Idyllwild on my lunch hour," I said, looking him in the eye, breathing deep, letting it out slow, gauging the effects of my words, "and I couldn't come back to school with my clothes all wet. So I went home."

Silence. We regarded each other across a chasm that grew wider by the second like two long-time foes who haven't met in several lifetimes.

"Did someone push you in?"

"No. I just slipped and fell in."

The first lie. The loss of innocence. The first move of the first battle of a long conflict. The first casualty of war is the truth. There would be no turning back, no retreat, no compromise. O what impossible situations arise when one leaves the freedom and beauty of mountains and moves to the cities and encounters ugly authority and distasteful bullies and stupid dress rituals and long, tiled, sterile hallways? Truth was the first casualty at RHS.

More silence.

"Are you surrrr-r-r-r-r-rrrrrrr you just fell in? Didn't someone push you?

"No."

"Well, Dick, perhaps I should tell you that we were informed that someone threw you in the pond. We know you were thrown in the pond. Now, don't be afraid of me. I want you to tell the truth."

Don't be afraid of him? I would have laughed had I not been so frightened, though it would be years before I could articulate that my instincts were warning me that my personal interests, happiness and integrity were not a priority of Mr. Rosaschi's and to fear as if the freedom of my soul depended on not getting caged by Rosaschi or his priorities.

"No one pushed me in. I got wet and went home."

"Well, Dick, there's a difference between falling in the pond and being pushed. If a student or students of this school threw you in the pond they should be punished. That sort of behavior is not acceptable. As a matter of fact, Dick, we know that certain members of the football team did throw you in the pond, and we can kick them off the football team for that."

"Why would you want to do that?"

"Are you saying they threw you in?"

"No."

"We both know you're not telling me the truth, Dick. And lying is not acceptable. Look, if you'll just tell me who was involved in the incident we can help you get back at them. We want to punish them."

"Why do you want to do that?

"Because the Senior Patrol overstepped its authority, and we can't allow that. We can't allow students to act this way. Now, dropping a few of those boys from the football team will teach them a lesson they won't forget, and we will be doing them a favor." Rosaschi smiled broadly and continued, "Otherwise, we can't accept the explanation that you fell in the pond and went home because you were wet. If that's your story we'll have no choice but to give you demerits for the classes you missed, and you'll be ineligible to participate in any school activities outside the classroom."

There it was. The mold was set for my high school career. I didn't know who was more repulsive to me at that moment--Rosaschi and his authority or the Senior Patrol bullies. As my good father was fond of saying, "Six of one, half dozen of another." It didn't seem like much of one, but I had a choice. I could align myself with Rosaschi and his authority and system, which I instinctively distrusted, disliked and rebelled against, or I could cover a pack of punk, teen-age, mush-headed, smirking bullies who had taught me through experience they were not to be trusted, admired, respected, liked or emulated. I might have sold out the football boys if circumstances and Rosaschi had been different, for I certainly owed the pigskinners nothing and felt no allegiance to them, but I chose instinct over experience for reasons I cannot explain. It set a pattern for making choices that has served me well.

I took a deep breath and let it out and privately thanked Chet Zoberski for his technical wisdom and looked Rosaschi in the eye so he would not doubt what I thought of him and said, "Well, Mr. Rosaschi, no one pushed me in the pond and I won't say that anyone did, and you can give me all the demerits you like."

I chuckled as I walked down the hall back to my class at the image in my mind of Rosaschi's face and the shock in his eyes after I said that. We understood each other, a distinct advantage for a 13 year old, but without really meaning to I had set myself apart from the mores and culture of my fellow freshman classmates and into a perpetual if low-grade guerrilla resistance with the administration of my high school. It took only a couple of days for the word to get out to the Senior Patrol and others what had happened, and both incidents (pond and Rosaschi) gave me a certain outlaw status in the high school community. So, in the perfect logic of the situation, I was invited to join the illegal 'fraternity' Delta Sigma, known as the Delts. (Bankofier was President.) The purpose of the Delts, so far as I could ever determine, was to achieve fellowship between members through re-enforcing the crude thinking and behavior of each other and getting as drunk as possible at weekly meetings in town and periodic beer busts held in the hills outside Reno. Other aspirations were mentioned, but I never achieved them through Delts and never observed their actualization in any of my Delt brothers.

A favorite Delta Sigma chant was called "Rough n' Tough Nevada Boys." It went like this:

> "We're rough n' tough Nevada boys.
> We're dirty sonsabitches.
> We wipe our ass
> With broken glass,
> And laugh because it itches.
> We fuck our wives
> With butcher knives,
> And that is but a trifle.
> We hang our balls
> On shithouse walls,
> And shoot 'em with a rifle."

That gives you an idea.

Eventually I found my own circle of friends and comrades, but without exception they were older so that each year of high school I had fewer close friends. By my senior year my best friends were gone to the University of Nevada, including my girl friend, and I spent most of my last high school year socializing with the University crowd. My high school experience was no more difficult or confusing or filled with angst than anyone else's, but the tone of that experience and much of my life was sounded that first week in Idyllwild Pond and the vice-principal's office. What I sought in life was always in the mountains and no one around me understood that, even when I told them. So I set about making the best of what I saw as a disagreeable situation and system without losing myself in the process. As with the rest of my classmates,

I found both success and failure in my inner quests and outward journey through Reno High School.

I took a course in typing and Father as always came through with more prescience than seems reasonable for his only son's needs. He indebted himself more than he could afford from his first Reno job as a carpenter to buy me a Royal portable typewriter for my 14th birthday. Father hated that job. I used the Royal for 30 years.

History as taught from the textbooks was never interesting to me until I learned to study it on my own and fill in the blank spots of the record as written by the victors and approved by their school boards. Reno High School American history classes never explored how or why the Paiute people wound up on a reservation by Pyramid Lake or that the land of the free and home of the brave was stolen from the indigenous peoples of America through the atrocious cowardice of genocide. Slavery in America was barely mentioned and its bastard child, institutional racism, was mentioned not at all. The best thing about Freshman history class was my class' brightest student, Garth Sibbold, a lank, thin boy with nearly transparent skin and blue eyes so aflame with information about the world that the sight of him turned my unspoken respect and admiration for his intellectual prowess into terror and shame at my own inadequate, limited, shameful, carnal and experiential knowledge of the same world. Though we were never friends I instinctively liked Garth, and it took me a couple of years before I realized he wasn't a saint and that he could use some rest, good food, sunshine, exercise and a friend a lot more than he could use another book, idea, fact, historical date, study hall or perfect grade. I grew to like the freshman history teacher, Anthony Zeni, for his ability to call on Garth, a 14 year old boy, to verify or come up with an historical fact Zeni had forgotten and then continue with class. It was a humble skill other, more authoritarian, teachers lacked. Zeni and Garth helped me get and see through the chimera of attaching respect to age and/or position without the substance respect demands. It was probably the most important thing I learned in high school history.

In every school system there are those who are completely involved in it while at the same time seeing right through it. Those are the true teachers in the American system of education and they are few and priceless. In the RHS athletic department the best of them was a physical education teacher, Bud Beasley, a small, graceful man with a huge nose and a big smile in a wrinkled face that made him look like the medieval court jester he undoubtedly was in another incarnation. A professional athlete in several sports, in the natural process of life he had turned to passing along his experience and knowledge and perspective to kids when he was too old to compete. He believed in the value of his own athletic life and loved teaching us how to appreciate and develop the potential of our own bodies, minds and spirits. I always wished he appreciated and knew how to ski but he did not. Though he was the best of the athletic department, like most traditional Nevada athletes of all ages of that time he viewed skiing as something a thin level above ballet dancing, cricket or curling. In mainstream Nevada culture athletics consisted of football (the king), basketball, baseball, track and field and boxing. Hunting and fishing were okay but even golf and tennis were suspect activities for males under thirty in Nevada's mainstream macho athletic culture. In a P.E. class one day we were playing touch football and I scored a touchdown with a couple of open field nifty fake moves. Bud complimented me on the run and asked why I hadn't tried out for the football team. I answered that skiing was my sport and that I didn't want to get hurt playing football. Even though I was the best known skier in RHS at the time, Bud said, "Well it's too bad you can't put that athletic ability to good use." So, while I liked Bud and very much respected him, I knew that in terms of my education, growth, potential and interests in life he was just another clueless adult to be dealt with the way one deals with a door to door salesman trying to sell you a bible or encyclopedia you neither want nor need. That is, with respect and politeness, warily and not very deep. And Bud was the best of RHS athletic educators. Others were, to my mind, much worse in intention, attention, competency and awareness.

One day Bud devoted an entire class to the skill of walking. A person must know how to walk before learning to run, he said, and none of us walked our own, natural walk. We all walked for an audience. Some guys were 'cool' and walked with slumped shoulders and a gait characterized by a slouch and feet lifted as little as possible above the earth and a heel lift that stopped briefly but noticeably halfway up before the step continued. These cool bobbers appeared to be stalking some unseen, unknown quarry, which in a certain sense they were. It was a popular gait of the '50s and I still see a few people practicing it. Perhaps the human gait never changes, only the context does.

Another noticeable walk was the lead heel gait. In this distinctive movement the walker, from laziness or oblivion or both, smashed the heel down first with a stiff leg which jarred the entire body and gave the walker a Frankenstein demeanor and likely caused some joint, muscle, ligament and even brain damage over time.

There was the jock walk, favored by body builders, football players and overweight toughs. It is recognizable by a puffed out chest, pulled back shoulders, thrust out chin, a perpetually pulled in, tense belly muscles, and could not be mistaken for the relaxed, natural attributes of good posture. The jock walk gave the jock walker a look of inflexibility which was often more than physically true. Naturally, in Nevada there were a few bow-legged cowboy walkers who at 14 had not spent enough years in the saddle to have earned bowed legs but who walked in imitation of fathers and other heroes to the rhythms of Tex Ritter, Gene Autry and the Lone Ranger. There were a few snobs who walked with a prissiness that reminded me of Principal Finch, as if it were slightly distasteful for them to actually touch the earth with their shod feet.

There was the country bumpkin/absent minded professor walk which varied in actual gait, but it was easily spotted in the unconscious demeanor of the walker with eyes focused on some problem of such complexity, depth and importance that the mundane social and bodily practicalities of life were irrelevant in the face of such concern. It was the walk of the deep thinker and the space case. And it was my walk, not because I thought or felt myself superior to my school mates (I was, for the most part, lonely and unsure of myself in a peer social sense), or because of any deep problem or cosmic idea inhabiting my mind and keeping me from paying attention to and acknowledging the present reality of now, nor did I float in the adolescent ozone level of the mind any more than the rest of my school mates. No, it was a huge insecurity about a physical problem that caused me to do the snob's walk. The problem was that I was near-sighted enough that anything more than three feet away progressively blended into a visual, flowing blur of rich color, vague shapes and indeterminate depth. Somehow--perhaps a John Wayne film or a careless or perverse quip from an adult I liked, respected or even loved--I had gotten it into my head that only 'sissies' wore glasses. When I realized at about age ten that my eyes had failed me I was humiliated, ashamed and outraged. My own body had let me down.

I wasn't going to be a sissy, whatever that was, no matter the cost, and I was able to hide my poor vision from the world until the eighth grade when a teacher figured out I couldn't read the blackboard. She marched me to the school nurse for an eye test I promptly failed and phoned my mother to reproach her for allowing a son to live in a world he could barely see. That my parents hadn't noticed that I couldn't see very well illuminates our relationship, but I caught hell from them when I got home from school that afternoon.

Soon I had eyeglasses I was mortified to wear, but being able to see in the classroom made school a lot more fun. Movies, which I had always loved, were even better: I was fascinated by the richness and clarity of form and color and at the interplay between characters and set that I'd missed when the silver screen was mostly a blur. And skiing, which was my salvation, opened up to me in myriad ways, changing my skiing and my sense of its magnificence. I could see what before I had only felt. Glasses changed my life and I loved what they could do for me.

Still, a sissy is a sissy, whatever that was. Many people I liked, respected, admired, trusted, emulated and loved (including my mother, a favorite uncle and a couple of very good skiers) wore glasses, but I was in the third year of high school before I had enough confidence to wear my own all the time. It is often said that image is everything and the matter of wearing glasses or not was my first lesson in the dynamics and consequences of the lack of confidence and self-respect that leads one to be more concerned with the shallowness of how one appears than with the depth of what one sees and, thereby, understands. This was a metaphor for a wide and dominant swath of the culture of Reno High School in the 1950s, and part of my adolescent education was the understanding that proxy selves were the norm and that it was a long path to the true self.

Chapter II
HIGH SCHOOL: SEX, DRUGS
AND ROCK 'N' ROLL

*"The sexual embrace can only be compared with music and
with prayer."*
Havelock Ellis

"In wine there is truth."
Pliny the Elder

*"The aim of life is to live, and to live means to be aware,
joyously, drunkenly, serenely, divinely aware."*
Henry Miller

At the end of my first year at RHS David Finch said
something that said it all. Harold's Club was the largest, most
successful casino in Reno at the time, famous for placing road
signs all over America with a simple message "Harold's Club
or Bust" and the exact road mileage from that spot to Harold's
Club. The Smith family which owned Harold's Club gave a
scholarship every year to one person from every high school in
Nevada. The scholarship was worth enough money to get that
student through four years of college to graduation at the
University of Nevada in Reno. Academic excellence and
economic need were among the criteria for winning a Harold's
Club scholarship. It was a prestigious, coveted and very useful
award which undoubtedly changed and enhanced the lives of
every one of its recipients, their families and their descendants.
Its only stipulations were that recipients maintain a high grade
point average and stay out of Harold's Club. The casino and its

scholarship were an integral part of and a clear benefit to Nevada culture and society.

At the graduation ceremonies for the class of 1953 one of Finch's duties was to give out the Harold's Club scholarship, which that year went to a friend who was both bright and deserving (and her first born a few years later became my goddaughter). Stiff as he was, Finch was a suitable suit for the job, and he gave all the appropriate accolades to both the worthy recipient and to this most prestigious, generous, beneficial scholarship given each year to a RHS graduate. Though he acknowledged that we all knew who the donor was he intoned that it was "not appropriate" to mentions the donor's name in a school setting, and he gave out the Harold's Club Scholarship without mentioning Harold's Club. The gambling industry and what it represented was not welcome in polite society or to be acknowledged in the minds of that society's children, though everyone at that graduation, including David Finch, lived directly or only a step or two removed from that industry. It was a defining moment for me, one that contributed to the development of an overly cynical, distrustful and at times self-destructive attitude toward society in general and its pillars in particular. American values, goals and social and cultural practices always have been and, it must be assumed, always will be severely conflicted. In no time or place in America's violent, Puritanical, slave-owning, imperialist history has this been more so than in Reno, Nevada in the 1950's. The roots of this conflict are deeper, older and more enduring than the concepts of America and Nevada, but inconsistency confuses the young whose radar for hypocrisy has not yet been completely blinded by compromise for the sake of parental approval and love, social/peer acceptance, unenlightened self-interest and, in some cases, basic survival. Since the 1930's the foundation of Nevada's economy and thereby its value system has been based on unlimited 24 hour a day gambling and drinking, legal prostitution, quick and easy divorce and quicker and easier marriage. That is, Nevada's economy exploits, promotes and profits from human weaknesses which, like human strengths, are part of the human condition. Nothing in history or current events gives any indication that human weakness is weakening its grip on human affairs, and there is nothing inherently wrong and probably a great deal right about geographic locales, social values and human economies based on recognizing, servicing and even exploiting that reality. Right or wrong, immoral or noble, under the rug or on the table, reality is not about to go away.

It is the illusion of things being other than they are that causes a disconnect between heart and mind, instinct and the social contract, human potential and the machinery of economy, personal integrity and community. It is the pretense that things are not what they are that binds and double binds the malleable minds and open hearts of young people trying to find and make their way. Nevada society in the 1950s was no worse or better than society in the rest of America, but its economic foundation took the cover off that society's pretenses and illusions, and then it pretended that it did not. From one perspective it was hilarious; from another it was frightening.

Little has changed.

A recent Las Vegas Chamber of Commerce promotion reads, "....the city's mystic qualities--the dazzling lights and glittering resorts where more than 35 million pleasure-seeking tourists wager millions of dollars every year...."

"Mystic qualities?" Las Vegas' mystic qualities?

"....where more than 35 million pleasure-seeking tourists wager millions of dollars every year."

The Chamber of Commerce forgot the part about the tourists wagering and losing millions of dollars every year.

Mystic qualities?

No wonder Jesus is said to have wept. Had he laughed with derision rather than weeping with sorrow more people might have paid attention. The burn of deserved mockery burns hotter, deeper and longer than an appeal to be considerate of another man's pain, deserved or not. Viewing society's professed mores and standards with skepticism has for the most part served me well, but when the skeptic is wrong he burns himself and I have.

There was truth, joy, contemplation, music, life without pretence and universal awareness in the world. I set out to find my share.

First, sex. Or, rather, first sex.

Mom and Dad weren't much help in finding out about sex. They didn't talk about such things. Because most of the places we had lived were small I had often heard their thrashing and groaning in the night, so I knew something amazing was up. Once my mother crawled into my bed in a drunken stupor mistake and started fondling me thinking I was Dad, but when she found out it was me she slurred "You're not Al" and bolted away to her own bed and Al. I was as confused as I imagine she was mortified. In the way of our family, the incident was never mentioned and I was an adult before it occurred to me that it should have been.

Despite the lack of discussion about human biology, such silence did not stop hormones from raging through the adolescent bodies of me and my buddies who talked about this thing called sex as if we knew something, but we didn't know much.

The folks weren't much help, but the schools were ridiculous. The definitive description of sex education in

America in the 1950's was written by Dan Wakefield and printed in Rolling Stone on October 9, 1975: "My first formal sex education in the classroom occurred my sophomore year in high school. I doubt that any of my classmates have forgotten it to this day. This sex education lecture came as part of a course titled 'Health and Safety...' We had been studying such mundane matters as basic first aid, traffic rules, personal hygiene and the bone structure of the body (like the leg-bone-connected-to-the-foot-bone and that sort of thing, but no mention of any sexual organs or how they functioned--they weren't included in the drawings we studied) and then one day the teacher announced that tomorrow the whole hour would be spent on the subject of sex. Naturally, we looked forward eagerly to the mysteries that would be revealed to us. At last! The straight poop on the subject, told to us by a teacher, right there in the high school classroom.

"When we went to class the next day the teacher waited until the bell had rung and all the class was seated. There was awesome silence. Miss Glammon, the teacher, was also known among the students as 'Mad Martha" for her rambling diversions and cracking of jokes. But on this day she was all business. First, she asked that all the girls leave the room, close the door behind them and wait quietly in the hall until she asked them to come back in. Once the classroom had been purged of all female students, Miss Glammon proceeded to pass around, for the examination of each male student, a series of color photos of the genitals of men afflicted with tertiary syphilis. As we carefully examined these diseased grotesqueries, she explained that this was what could happen as a result of sex.

"When each of us had examined the pictures, she asked that the boys now leave the room and wait in the hall while the girls came in.

"In the hall a couple of guys tried to joke, but most of us looked greenish gray, and I found myself, alone with some others, trying unobtrusively to feel down between my legs and make sure everything was all right.

"The girls were shown the same sort of pictures, only of women in the same condition. They were also taught the same lesson about the pictures.

"That was the sum total of classroom instruction in sex for the 1950 graduating class of Shortridge High School, widely renowned as one of the finest public high schools in the nation."

Thanks, Dan.

No wonder the adult world was viewed with alarm, distrust and even disdain by me and many but by no means all of my peers. Fortunately, formal education did not preclude and was in my circle of friends secondary to reality education. Formal education was based on fear of retribution, punishment and lack of authority and peer approval.

Reality education could be fearful and scary but it was based on personal experience. Reality education was real.

I don't remember how I came to be invited, much less how my parents allowed it to happen, but I joined three older RHS boys on a 600 mile weekend road trip to Ely, Nevada for the Reno-Ely football game which Reno won 74-0 with its outsized team of man/boys like Manoukian, DiRicco, Bankofier and others. There were no speed limits in Nevada in those days and we drove to Ely and back often at over 100 mph, drinking beer, tossing empty bottles and cans out the car windows and in general acting like irresponsible, drunken teenagers on a spree. Appropriately enough in a state where prostitution was and is legal, I got laid for the first time in my 13 years in the Big-4 whore house, Ely's finest, by a 45 year old saggy-breasted, flabby bodied, red haired old whore who made me feel so good that I loved her with all the truth of the four dollars it cost and the perfect, impeccable feelings she raised in me and gave my life. I tingled with fright as she took my hand and led me along a dim hall to her double bed room with orange-red-purple bedspread and a shaded lamp on a stand giving off diffused, erotic light that was perfect for exchanging the questionable virtue of virginity for the undeniably consequential world of sex. My heart was beating like thirty blacksmiths when she told me to take my clothes off which I did faster than you can say "hard-on" and I had one quivering with excitement and anticipation and adventure. I was standing naked by the bed with my erection and feeling foolish as hell when she reached under her bed and introduced me to the peter pan, which is not a little boy who never grew up, though the word play is wonderful, but, rather, a porcelain bowl filled with warm water into which she plunged my tingling prick to wash it off, a ceremony she performed both before and after the act of the fuck. I might have ejaculated in her hand but the disappointment would have killed me. The damnedest thing happened after she dried off my throbbing bobbing penis and I sat on the bed to await my first lady and watch her undress. She was fumbling around in her ear buried in red, frizzy hair when I asked her, "Hey, what's your name," and got no answer so I asked again just as she turned around and saw I was speaking. "Heh, Sonny, what did you say?" she said. "Excuse me, but I took off my hearing aid and I don't hear so good."

And so she had. The old bird was standing there with a hearing aid in her hand. The ridiculous humor of the situation buried my fear, nervousness, excitement and even my sensitized pecker. There I was, a boy about to lose virginity with a worn out old woman ten years older than my own mother, and she can't even hear me ask her name. I exploded with laughter and the old girl, whose name I never learned saw the humor in it too, bless her, and her flabby belly and droopy breasts jiggled with laughing joy and she jumped on the bed with the grace of a young girl. "C'mere," she said, and pulled me down upon her and into her and we fucked for several eternities and the unmentioned jewel within the perfect privacy of my freely shared feelings opened up like sunflowers in the morning sun with all the colors of the universe.

Later, when we were getting dressed and she had her hearing aid back in she asked, "Was this your first time?"

"Yes. Did I do alright?"

"You did fine, Sonny, you did fine." She smiled a beautiful, friendly, tired old whore's smile that I loved and took with me into the changed world of the Ely night and my friends who had also gotten laid. Everything was subtly different. First sex for me was not romantic, but in a way that childhood could not understand I was no longer a boy. It was obligatory to talk about the experience with my friends, but it was impossible to describe the real erudition of the feelings created (from the loss of innocence?) or the entirely new perspective that was mine to grow with. And I did.

While formal education was based on fear and provided some tools for staying out of trouble, reality education led to joy. Sometimes it did not lead to joy but at least it was a possibility. Reality trumps formality every time, though it must always be kept in mind that one man's reality is another man's nightmare, and, of course, still another man's dream.

Live your life running from fear or live your life in the pursuit of joy. That was the primary message of Reno High School's curriculum.

Fear or joy. Take your pick.

Mainstream America's drug of choice is alcohol and always has been. By the time I arrived at Reno High School I was an experienced drinker. The first time I drank I was 11. The first time my parents caught me drunk I was 12. We drank beer for the most part, but my first drink at 11 was a gin and tonic made for me by our summertime Zephyr Cove neighbor Howie Norton, 4 years my senior and a ski racing friend for many years. My parents were heavy drinkers in those years, though Dad backed off considerably about the time we moved to Reno. Mom, however, was an alcoholic to her grave. My family on both sides of the gene pool as far back as I have investigated (several generations) is littered with alcoholics. Whether the attraction to drugs is genetic, familial, societal, cultural, or a matter of personal character, I grew up in a world and family of drinkers. So did many of my friends and peers. In Nevada in the 1950's, drinking was as prevalent among teen-agers as it was among their parents, though few ever drank together. So far as I know no study has ever been done on the correlation between teen age drug/alcohol use and that of the parents, but instinct and common sense indicates that it exists. The best story I know about this association involves the great French painter Maurice Utrillo, who was committed to the bottle at an early age and to an institution for alcoholism at the tender age of eleven. Maurice was started on his vaporous path to truth by his incredible mother, Suzanne Valadon, herself an artist of considerable skill and insight. She was also beautiful, a model, a lover and friend to several of the community of Parisian artists at the end of the 19th century. It has been suggested that the grand master of impressionism, Auguste Renoir, was Utrillo's father, but his genealogy has never been established. Suzanne loved the night life of Paris and never had enough money for such luxuries as baby sitters, but she came up with an ingenious solution to the problem. Whenever she wanted to go out at night, which were most nights, Suzanne would stuff a rag into a bottle of wine, lay the bottle on its side next to baby Maurice, and let the lad suck on the wine soaked rag. That gave the boy something to do and put him right to sleep with no fuss, and a bottle of cheap French burgundy kept Maurice out of trouble for many nights. Like every solution to a problem, it had its consequences. By five Utrillo had dropped the rag and was plugging straight from the bottle. By nine he was reeling around the streets of Paris like a good clochard, a topic of gossip and concerned conversation in certain circles of Parisian society. By eleven he was being put away in institutions for enforced drying out. For ten years he was dried out and filled up so many times that by twenty Suzanne had given up incarcerating him in places he did not want to be. A mother's love knows no bounds, they say, an avowal more true than the appalling parenting skills of Suzanne would allow most people to accept. She came up with another obvious if unorthodox solution to the problem of dealing with alcoholism in a young man trying to find his way in the unorthodox world of the artist--she made an artist of him. One sunny day not long after Utrillo (a name given him by a Spanish friend of Suzanne's who history has never given serious consideration as the father) came home from a particularly difficult drying out session, Suzanne set him down before a canvas with some oils and told him to paint. "Paint!" she said. Cold turkey. Not even a drawing lesson for a warm up. He must have learned something from a lifetime of Suzanne and her artist friends and the museums and galleries of Paris, but so far as anyone else knew or he ever said Utrillo never before drew a line or painted a stroke. "Paint!" she ordered, and he did. He also drank. He began both endeavors under the tutelage of his mother in the classic mold of child rearing. Suzanne became, as she grew more aware of how deep went his involvement, how high flew his talent in both endeavors she had started him upon, amazed. As a mother she was pretty upset about his alcoholism. As an artist she was delighted with his genius for painting streets and buildings and boulevards and trees and windows and the strange, stick-like figures who represent human beings in his colorful, existential paintings that are warm and moving even if all the people in them seem added on as an afterthought. I suspect they were. Perhaps he felt as if the creation had added humans as a sodden afterthought to the landscape. Whatever his thoughts, Utrillo drank and painted with unremitting energy until he died at the age of 87, having lived his life to the cork according to the only two lights his mother ever gave him with enough desperation to make him believe she really meant it--wine as baby sitter, painting as therapy. Not bad. Many mothers of a more traditional and conservative bent have done worse for their children.

I don't think that any of my friends at school were sucking down wine in the cradle, but Suzanne Valadon's parenting skills were only different in degree, not substance, from those of many of my friend's parents, including mine. If alcohol was good enough for Mom and Dad and good enough for generations of Reno tourists who dearly love Nevada's 24 hour bars, it was good enough for us. If there is a more obvious reason for young people drinking I am not aware of it.

Except in extreme cases like Utrillo's, kids do not usually drink alone. Solo drinking is an adult endeavor. Teen age drinking/drugging is a peer driven activity and I cherished my friends and wanted their respect and approval. Friends are to life what the oasis is to the desert traveler. Some people spend their lives in the oasis. Others spend their lives moving along the trackless paths of the endless desert, secure in the knowledge that the oasis is always there. One of life's sad experiences is to return to a trusted watering hole to find it dried up, poisoned, unrecognizable or turned into friendship's version of a McDonald's hamburger joint. One of the joys of life is reuniting with an old friend after a long expedition into the unknown, returning with riches from another land after eluding posses of insane vigilantes, or just returning to the oasis with holes in your shoes, tattered clothes and psyche, a brain full of impossible adventures and a heart thirsting for the clear waters of friendship.

I found several friendships that first high school year; some remain, some have disappeared, all remain a part of my life.

For reasons having to do with the lifestyle I had known as a young boy at Lake Tahoe and the fact that I was bigger and looked older than my age, the friends I made in Reno were older. This put more strain on my capacities than I could naturally accept. A year of maturity in the early teens is enormous, and I was outmatched and over my head in nearly everything I was doing with my friends. I chose the position of extremist to keep up. If we were drinking beer I always drank the most, and by the time I was 15 I had earned a reputation as a drinker. Skiing was the main focus of my energies and when we competed I pushed hard and naturally excelled, and I gained a reputation as a skier as well.

Drinking was an integral part of social life, usually with male friends, less often with girl friends and rarely with girls who were just friends. On weekend nights we sometimes rode around town or parked in the desert to drink beer and discuss philosophical questions: Why a beer can opener was called a "church key." Why girls were such a problem. What we wanted to do and what kind of adults we wanted to become in that far off time when maturity would crash upon us like a meteor from the heavens. Why boys could be drafted at 18 but could not vote or legally drink. Why girls were not drafted. Why some school classes were stultifying dull while others were engrossing. Why Idel Anderson, my French teacher, hated me. We hid from a disapproving adult world in our cars for much of our drinking, and sometimes one of us would have a parentless house for a day or night or two and we would gather there in comfort and privacy to talk and drink. We were not so different from our fathers and mothers who gathered in bars and living rooms and back yards to drink and discuss the things of their lives through the lens of truth provided by their drug of choice. Though we were 'under' age and not supposed to drink, we did. Our role models disapproved of us doing what they did, and sometimes their disapproval was extreme and ugly The philosophical question of whether that disapproval was hypocrisy and fear or care and love was endlessly discussed, and the people who could/should/might (or not) have contributed the most to the conversation and a better understanding of life were never invited. Just as our parents wouldn't have dreamed of inviting their children to have a beer or three with them, we wouldn't have considered inviting any of our parents to a party.

That dynamic is the basis for drug education in America, and it has evolved to what is called today "the war on drugs." As in all wars, there are no winners.

I went to school dances and had a few dates but skiing was my main outlet for the energy of adolescence. I really looked forward to the RHS Ski Team for several reasons, among them the fact that I'd never had a real ski coach before. I anxiously looked forward to the benefits of his expertise, and at first it worked out very well. During the pre-season dryland training we ran, hopped, jumped, exercised and stretched and sweated like devils each day after school under the tutelage of the coach, Les Hawkins. I had never before conditioned my body through systematic discipline. The experience was hard and it worked and self-discipline became a life-long and good friend. The core of the boys RHS Ski Team in 1953 was Bob Lerude, Lynn Johnson, Bud Sorensen and me. Bob and Lynn were seniors, Bud was a junior and I was a freshman. We were all friends and had a great time that season--skiing, racing, traveling, partying, and learning about life. Though I was the youngest I had the best results, and the team had a successful season against the other high school teams. Skiing was the most important (possibly substantial) aspect of my life, as it was not for the others. My self-image and relationship to my community of peers was very tied up with ski racing, and because of its importance to my life it was not surprising I had the best results. Athletes in high school who excelled in their sport were awarded a 'letter' sweater or coat with the letter R. To 'letter' in a sport was a mark of accomplishment, a badge of honor and a very cool thing to wear around school and town. No RHS freshman had earned a letter in many years and as I had clearly earned it I looked forward to my letter sweater and the status and, more important to me, acceptance into the community of RHS it conferred.

Les Hawkins, a RHS English teacher, was a good but not fine skier and a shy, decent man of little apparent passion about anything. We quickly learned he knew less about ski racing than we did, a lack of knowledge as obvious to the team as it was, I suppose, to Les. As a consequence, we more tolerated than listened to Les as a ski coach. I was the worst offender of patronizing Les as I was the hungriest for knowledge about skiing, and our coach trying to teach me the intricacies of ski racing was to, my young mind, ludicrous. Les was doing his job and I was pursuing a passion. If I had had a different attitude towards authority, been more mature, had a more generous spirit or even been clearer about the difference between politeness and obsequiousness Les and I might have worked out a healthy relationship. But I didn't and neither did we. I didn't want him waxing my skis or showing me a line in a race course or advising me on racing technique. I didn't dislike him but I didn't believe he knew what he was doing or talking about and never took him seriously as a ski coach. I constantly sought out the few people around Reno who were more experienced in ski racing, usually professional skiers, for advice and direction. Not all of what I picked up from those advisors was beneficial or correct, but that is another story. Les was the authority, the coach, the leader of the ski team and I was the guiltiest of not recognizing him as such. What I wanted from Les was to be left alone, but I unintentionally offended him with a thousand cuts that bled resentment, something I would not understand for many years.

At the end of that first ski season, after all the ski meets with other schools were over, Les called me into his office. He got right to the point. In a calm, serious tone, as if speaking to someone he had never met, Les informed me that despite being the best skier on the RHS ski team that year he had decided I would not be awarded a letter. Despite my results in the races I did not deserve it, he said.

I asked why.

He answered that he had received reports that I had been seen drinking and that athletes who drank did not deserve letters.

Who had seen me drinking, I asked.

He could not say.

Had anyone else on the team been seen drinking, I asked.

No, just me.

Was I the only ski team member who would not get a letter that year, I asked.

Yes.

Something almost but not quite physical escaped my body right then, like a ghost exiting a room, and I knew immediately it would never be back and that I was diminished by its loss. I was 14 years old.

I looked directly at Les, trying hard not to let him see what I had just lost or how I felt. "That's not right, Les, and you know it," I said. "So long, Asshole." His incredulous eyes showed several levels of shock. I walked out of his office without another word, as angry and hurt as I knew how to be, half expecting him to follow and demand apology or inflict retribution. I think that if he had so much as mentioned my name or followed me I would have turned on and hit him as hard and as long and as much as I possibly could. But he neither followed me nor spoke and I walked blindly down the sterile halls of RHS fighting back tears like never before. In the many years after that meeting that I knew and skied and dealt with Les Hawkins I never looked directly at him again.

There were three more years at RHS during which I did all the usual and a few unusual things high school kids in America do. I had friends and girl friends and good teachers and bad, but I never managed to feel connected to the community of Reno High School. The best teachers I had were Blythe Bulmer, my English teacher for the last three years of high school, Rex Daniels, the journalism teacher, Miss Ernst, the geometry teacher, and John Marino, the science teacher. The worst was Idel Anderson, the French teacher. I learned plenty from them all. But the major life lessons that most affected my life and its path were picked up early on from such diverse teachers as the Senior Patrol--Bankofier, DiRicco, Manoukian, Keever--and Rosaschi, Finch, Beasley, Hawkins, an old whore in Ely with a hearing aid, a Royal typewriter, Zeni, Sibbold, my friends and the mountains and snow and world of skiing. Reality education at its best.

END BOOK TWO

BOOK THREE

Chapter I
SKIING

*"It is better to go skiing and think of God than go to church
and think of sport."*
Fridtjof Nansen

*"Powder snow skiing is not fun. It's life, fully lived, life lived in
a blaze of reality."*
Delores LaChapelle

In September 1963, just over 11 years after father dropped
me off in the Reno High School parking lot for the first day of
school I set a world record for speed on skis in Portillo, Chile,
traveling just over 171 kilometers an hour (106 miles per hour).
It was a defining experience and the apex of a ski racing career
that was both frustrating and fulfilling, but it was neither the
culmination nor the most meaningful encounter with self-
knowledge in a skier's life. Ski racing was wonderful and for
many years the focus of most of my energies, but it (and I)
suffered from the same social and personal dynamics that
marked my relationships with mainstream social mores as
exemplified at RHS, authority in general and my difficulties in
getting anger and rebellion out of my own way. I had my fair
share of success and failure as a ski racer, but at that time speed
skiing was so far out of the mainstream of skiing that its lack of
organization, authority figures and entrenched protocols, to say

nothing of the pure joy (and terror) of discovering just how fast you could go on a pair of skis, made it the perfect means of expression for me. After an entire ski racing career dealing with people like Les Hawkins, the politics of junior ski racing, university ski team (where at one time Hawkins was also the coach), the more convoluted politics of national ski racing and the torturous maze of authoritarian political chicanery that marked the U.S. Ski Team (and, so far as I can tell, still does), discovering speed skiing was like drinking from a fresh, cold mountain spring on a hot day.

Speed skiing was freedom in action.

My good friend Ron Funk and I went to Chile in June 1963 specifically to set a record and we were joined in our endeavor by our North American ski racing comrade C.B. Vaughan after we got there. Ron organized the attempt with Henry Purcell who owned Portillo and helped us enormously and became a life-long friend and a couple of friends in the Chilean Ski Federation. It required a huge amount of work on our part to make the track smooth enough for a record. Ron broke his leg two months into the three month process of getting the track and ourselves up to the highest speeds and couldn't participate on the last, best, fastest day. I wrote of that day in my book "The Straight Course":

"The process of detachment--of viewing myself abstractly--had reached an astonishingly intricate, fragile state. I was in an incredible state of mind. Fear, desire, frustration, the scope of our attempt, and pure physical and mental exhaustion had combined to wind me up so tight, so fast, that the contest was not as much with time as whether the record or the human mechanism would fall first.

"The next day, the twenty-ninth, was the last possible day Portillo would be open, the last possible chance for the record. Accordingly, we decided to go up early in the morning and run while the track was still ice. We were sure ice would make the difference. With one day, perhaps only one run left and in us, it was necessary to extend ourselves. Sleep, the night of the twenty-eighth, was restless and unfulfilling. Fatigue sleep of a job undone.

"We rose early, ate, and were out on the hill while most of the hotel slept. It was cold and clear. The shaded track was rock hard. Springtime frozen corn; it would remain firm for several hours. We had prepared the track perfectly at the end of the previous day. For the first time, every condition was in our favor.

"We took a practice run to test the timing from 20 yards above the measured area. We averaged more than 100 kilometers per hour, and I knew in the center of my spine our track was as ready as we. I would not allow the thought that it was more ready.

"The sun began to climb the track. C.B. and I went with it. Because of the steepness, 400 meters takes great amounts of time and energy, and I was very tired. We climbed slowly, planning to reach the top before the sun exposed the entire track. I felt C.B. had more energy than I, but that may have been hypersensitivity to my own state.

We talked and joked, but the next day we could not remember any of it. When we got to the top the sun was on the track. Portillo was awake. Far below--an impassable distance--people came out to watch. On the hotel porch many had binoculars. Skiers came down the plateau and stood off to one side near the bottom of the track. Spectators of a play in which the actors had not learned their parts, an audience removed, but only on the surface of action. They feared and hoped as did we. Difficult to realize at that moment, but we needed and used their positive energy; for it is true that each is a part of the main.

"In that critical state and time, reality was C.B., the gigantic track below, the feeling of vertigo, and the hard knowledge that the next few minutes were the culmination of all that was behind, the determinant of much of what lay ahead. Funk, Purcell, the timers, other racers and many friends were down there watching with varying degrees of interest and involvement; our friends; warm human beings with whom we had formed close and not so close relationships, laughed, danced, drank, gotten angry, forgave and were forgiven; our immediate companions in eating, sleeping, working, relaxing--life; but at the top of the Portillo speed track, those people might as well have been on another planet. All living, except my reality, was suspended. They could not really understand the high degree of control we had made from the chaos of our feelings, nor our predicament, nor the mind which equates self-abstraction with being near God. They could only see us as tiny figures on a white wall of snow, but the least thoughtful could not help but realize our commitment.

"I was nearly sick with vertigo and fear. We did warm up exercises (a delicate task on a slope of 45 degree steepness), and in those last minutes I discovered a bit of the structure of action. The months of discipline, work, self-abstraction and the winding up process, honed to a fine, sharp edge by the last run on the last day under the iciest, most difficult, most perfect conditions enabled me to see myself marvelously clear.

"I nearly laughed and would have but for physical fear. A great calm and confidence (not in **success**, but in my **self**) filled me. 'Duped again,' I would say in a later time. I was at the precipice of the fastest skiing ever done, the fastest a human body had moved without free-falling or mechanical aids, hanging on the side of a snow-blasted cliff, stinking with fear and the stubbornness not to be beaten by it, when I saw the absurdity of my position. Many things had put me up to where

I was--whatever it was in my inherent personality that caused me to recognize skiing as my form of expression when a young boy had put me there, and a racing potential which eluded my best efforts. And a public school education with its accent on grade rather than content. And the power of the great yellow lie called journalism which warps the world's mind with its pretension and shallowness. And the Hollywood ethic upon which I was weaned, an ethic preaching that what matters is coming through in the end--a barely disguised belief in a better life after death which makes light-headed excuses for lifetimes of misery. And people like Number 7 (a man who managed to keep me out of an Olympic qualifying race to which I was entitled to compete) who wages war on the past with inverted minds. And all the sweet experiences that had gone to hell. And Bob Beattie (U.S. Ski Team Head Coach with whom I had differences) with his clumsy feet and blind assurance. And all the teams I and others would never make. And all the old ski racer friends like Marvin Moriarity and Gardner Smith and Jim Gaddis who had been caught by the sharp, sly, double-edged axe of politics, wielded by the universal soldiers of my particular way of life...but there was also the strength that learning about those kinds of things gives. And there were the good examples of how a man should be; I had once categorized them according to three fine competitors--Bud Werner, Ralph Miller and Dick Buek. There was Funk down there taking pictures, broken leg and all his hopes. There was my wonderful aunt Marcelle, dying the hard way. And my friends Barnes, Lyder and Tiger, already gone. And my parents who never understood but took pleasure when it reached newsprint. There was the good life and people of La Parva. And there were all the friends right there at Portillo. Somewhere in the world was a guy I didn't know named Plangger, and he had something (the world record at 168 kph) I wanted. And with me was my comrade C.B. Vaughan. All the people and times and places I had known, and all the shades of emotion I had ever felt, and all the work I had ever accomplished came with me to Portillo. Pushed, pulled, or just came along as disinterested observers. Hard to know, but assuredly there.

"And every one of them copped out at the last minute, leaving me entirely, flat alone. Duped again. Abandoned by my own illusions, leaving **just** me to do whatever was necessary.

"The essential education.

"The territory my mind had chosen as its battling ground--my place to wage war on all the inequity, hypocrisy, stupidity, and frustration I had ever known; and my time to justify myself for Marcelle, Ken, Tiger, Brett, Brunetto, Funk, Llewellyn, and to my particular friends in Reno, Ron the mustache, and Joan the potter, and to a few others for their faith, friendship, and a smile at the right time--was an icy, precipitous piece of snow on the side of an Andean mountain, useful in nature only for the tiny bit of water it would hold a little longer. Absurd. Pathetic in its attempt. Yet, something would be saved. Something communicated all around. Duped again, but not entirely for nothing.

"I could have laughed.

"Inside, where action begins, I was peaceful, confident, and supremely happy. Calm, because preparation gives self-control, and I had come prepared. Confident, because confidence is the only possible state of mind under such circumstances; to be where we were without believing in ourselves would be suicidal, and, while life **is** richer and more poignant when it is risked (an effect carrying over and preceding the act of risking), it is so through a deep desire to go on living. And happy, supremely so, I say, to discover in that structure mentioned earlier, that life was okay, and so was I; the important thing was commitment, and I found in myself the ability to give everything, to lay the whole show on the line. In that ability is hidden happiness, and all men have it, lurking somewhere amidst neuroses, education, experience, belief and centered in the heart. Success, while certainly not unimportant, is a problematical (mathematical) afterthought.

"While in that delicate, beautiful state, I adjusted my goggles one more time, and signaled my readiness to the timers, feeling more than usual action in the center of things. Far below (like looking through the wrong end of a telescope) the signal pole waggled back and forth. I wished C.B. luck and said I'd see him at the bottom. I felt a sentimental reluctance to leave the big redhead up there alone.

"'Good luck, Boy,' he said. C.B. called his friends 'Boy.'

"I planted my left pole below and to the back of my skis, the right above and to the front, executed a quick jump turn, pulled my poles out in midair, and landed in a full tuck, headin' down.

"Acceleration like a rocket launched in the wrong direction. The sound of endless cannons, moving closer. Irreversible commitment.

"The soles of my feet said this was the one. My eyes saw the transition and peaceful flat, far, far away. My body, appalled at the danger in which it had been placed, acted automatically, reluctantly perhaps, but with an instinct and precision that preceded the mind which put it there. My naked mind had finally gotten hold of the big one that had always gotten away.

"Jesus, it is fast.

"After 100 meters I estimate the speed at over 150 kph. That left 200 meters to the timing and 100 meters in the trap before the longed for landing. Never have I wanted more to be finished with something. A few seconds, less than ten....a long way, more than time can record. More than anything, I wanted not to fall. Probably there is little difference in the end result of a fall at 150 kph and one at 170 kph, but the ice that morning accentuated everything that was happening. Acceleration. Sound. The beating against the legs. The texture feeling. The thin line of error.

"In big speeds the skis make peculiar movements. On ice they make them faster, harder. Tremendous air pressure pushes the tips up; the skis want to become airborne. You push forward with everything you have. The air pushes up the tips; you push forward; there is a continuous change of pressure from tip to tail of the skis. Continuous and violent. On a good run your body absorbs both change and violence. On a bad run your body demonstrates them. The tips tend to make a curious, fishtail motion, which, combined with the tip to tail pressure change, cause the ski to pivot slightly underneath the foot. These things are happening to the skis you are riding. Happening as fast as a vibration and with as much power as the speed you are carrying.

"While this is happening at the feet the rest of the body is trying to hold a stable, compact, tuck position. Air pressure tries to push you over backward, with a continuous, ever mounting force. If you break the tuck the pressure tries to rip your arm off. If you stood up at those speeds, your back would hit the snow before the thought could come of what a mistake you had just made.

"About a hundred yards above the trap, my right arm, as it had the previous day, flew out to the side for some inexplicable reason of balance. It is tremendously unsettling. (The next time you are ripping along one of America's scenic highways at 100 mph, stick an arm out the window.) I jammed both hands forward and down--a high speed version of what, in another age, was known at the 'Sailer crouch,' the most stable position in skiing--and rocketed through the trap and into the transition.

"Each mile per hour after 95 feels like a difference of 10 miles per hour at half that speed. When I reached the transition I felt more like a Ferrari than a human, and I knew before the timers that no one had skied that fast before.

"The run-out was easy--gradually extending the arms and raising the body for air drag, and a long left turn entered at about 60 mph until I was able to stop. It took a couple hundred more feet than any previous run.

"I stopped. I took off my helmet and goggles. I was alive. The most alive I had been in my twenty-four years. I felt the sun and saw the beauty of Portillo in the Andes as never before. My spirit was clean. My mind could rest content. I had discovered my own structure of action, and I had acted. For the time, the illusions had been stripped away, and I was completely alive. Also, successful.

"I walked back around the corner and halfway up the flat. Up on the hill, Funk was jumping up and down with his cast like a club-foot chimpanzee.

"'One-seven-one,' he yelled. 'Wahooo,' hopping about like mad, arms waving.

"I stood in the flat waiting for C.B. The calm joy I was experiencing was tempered by anxiety for the big redhead. I was safe in a giant, flat expanse of snow; I was alive; I was happy; I was tuned to a very high plane; but it wasn't over until C.B. was safely down, so I waited a little longer.

"Despite fatigue, the aftereffects of hyper-adrenalation, anxiety and realization of the world record with its attendant hoopla, those few minutes were the most peaceful, satisfying moments I had ever known. I knew they would be few, and I knew they were enough.

"In ten minutes the diplomatic 'Bobby' Muller and Chalo Dominquez, the timers, had reset the watches. The pole waved for 'Ceb.' He came in his yellow-black racing tights like a tiger falling off a white cliff. The sound--skis rattling against ice, wind rippling skin-tight clothes, and the impact of a body moving through air at 100 mph--carried clear to the flat; a unique sound impossible to forget, and not a reassuring one. C.B. rode a tight but high tuck. Twice his arms broke position, flashing out to his sides and immediately returned. Then, quite literally, he thundered into the transition and past me on the flat and around the corner to a stop.

"It was all over.

"I stood within my peace, wondering about C.B.'s time and looking to see if it was in me to go up again that day, in case his time was faster than mine. Almost two years later I was to remember that moment; I remembered it because it took that long to understand what that moment, that question and impetus in my self was. As luck would have, it was a catechism I was not to face that day.

"C.B. was still around the corner, experiencing, discovering, and questioning on his own when Tito Beladone, the Grand Ambassador of Chilean skiing and friend of several years, skied down the outrun to me. 'You and C.B. have the same time,' he said. The moment was inordinately formal to Tito's vision of skiing, but he gave me a hug, a pat on the back, a kiss on the cheek, Chilean fashion, and his congratulations. He was elated and proud; I felt humble to have a part in giving him that moment.

"I thanked Tito and skied down to C.B. I told him what had happened and we had a few minutes together. During those minutes we knew what we had accomplished, and it was a fine time. Then the backwash of success arrived. The friends, the ones with faith, the interested, the incredulous, and even the cynical and weak doubters, came to say what we already knew. And it was wonderful to hear."

The essential education.

It was a great education, but it had begun long before Portillo and was far from over. I had always seen skiing as much more than the competitive, comparative and the far edge of extreme. If you stay too long too close to any edge that thin it will eventually crumble and kill you or leave you with nothing more than memories. Memories can be wonderful, but they are not the stuff of life.

LaChapelle found life in powder snow skiing. I found life in skiing--in powder, on ice, in a race course, bumps, the back country, corn snow and crud. Skiing is life--"life, fully lived, life lived in a blaze of reality." The act of skiing and the stage on which it takes place are both beautiful in the same way that music and the musician are beautiful. Putting into words the experience of skiing is a bit like trying to describe making love: words may indicate but can't convey the feelings, meanings or the sensuous life of action. At best they create empathy and, perhaps, inspire the reader to find out for him or her self. These words are intended to show some limitations of the word. On one level skiing combines the physical control of the body in movement with the sensuality of riding upon a carpet of frozen white water and the visual/spiritual aesthetic of being outside in the mountains in wintertime. The purest words can only indicate, never re-create the visceral, sensual, aesthetic experience of the sun reflected a trillion times by bonded snow flakes, each flake, like each person, refracting/reflecting the light according to its unique design and qualities. The cold, hostile mountain air can kill, and the same air gives life breathed into lungs with clean gulps of honest reminders of how fragile is the balance, how exquisite the foundation. There is in skiing the blaze of reality slamming into a turn with all the forces of gravity, momentum, balance, muscular and mental coordination, education and strength in harmony. Perfect harmony with its unstated possibility that in making the turn makes you capable of creating a harmonious life, and in that present instant of controlled harmony are turning dreams into reality. To focus with all your being on the subtlety of pressure on the edge of a ski continuously in the process of change, sometimes with a power that could break bones, sometimes with the force of a snowflake landing on a windless day, sometimes with both at the same time, is to turn concentration into meditation, action into life at its freest and best.

Describable or not, skiing was the first love of my life. It set me free from the weird things other people could do to your person, and nothing and no one could compete with it. Skiing is fun and it is simple--me, sometimes a few friends, snow, mountains, skis. I trusted the elements implicitly as I did not trust many adults and even fewer of the channels an adult world left open to flow along with its sanction. Skiing was beautiful. The adult world wasn't. This perspective was as simple as it proved to be simplistic. As I grew into adulthood I learned that the causes of my childhood angers were tones of colors and shades of gray, not black and white. It was a long time before I knew that most people do the best they can and that their failings are more those of ignorance and experience than lack of care or love. Mountains were neither ignorant nor wise. They were impartial and gave and took in fair measure, and I embraced them with fervency. In a sense, skiing saved my life by giving me a mechanism and the strength to carry around those trunks of angry baggage without dumping them on the world in sociopath rage. Skiing has given me a great life and helped me unload some of that baggage in the form of social criticism. Whether that criticism has been beneficial or destructive depends, I suppose, on one's perspective; but it seems to me that criticism tempers and makes stronger both individuals and society. Blind acceptance weakens and blinds and makes them dangerous.

In 1949 my schoolmate and boyhood friend Doug Gaynor borrowed his sister's skis for me to use and one day we hiked up and skied down and hiked up and skied down and hiked up and skied down a hill in Tahoe Valley until dark. By the end of the day and after many falls me and my first love were wedded for life, for better or worse, for richer and poorer, all in abundance as it proved. Doug was my first teacher and was a fellow competitor and friend for many years after this first day on skis. Within a week I had badgered my parents into getting me a pair of my own skis they could not really afford. Within a year I was the Far West Ski Association 4-event (downhill, slalom, jumping, cross-country) champion in the under 14 age group. After this competition my parents drove me to Reno to the studio of Ernie Mack, the best ski and portrait photographer in that part of Nevada, to have my portrait taken, such was their pride in and support of my first skiing accomplishment. This 1950 studio photo shows me at 11 holding my first trophy, dressed in a ski sweater my aunt Esther knitted, baggy ski pants held up by a belt buckle won in the races, lace ski boots, and a shy, pleased smile on my face. It would be decades before I would appreciate the rarity of my good fortune, through the grace of my childhood friend, of finding my path in life before I was a teen-ager. Skiing was my destiny and I knew it at an early age. I was deep into adulthood before recognizing how difficult and, in all too many cases, impossible for other people to acknowledge, respect, deal with or understand life lived in my reality.

In those first winters at Tahoe, living in Tahoe Valley, Stateline and Zephyr Cove, I managed to ski an hour or two most days after school and all day on weekends. At one point I had built a jump hill and packed out a slalom course less than a hundred yards from the house in Zephyr Cove. I climbed up and skied down them both in a Sisyphusian frenzy until dark nearly every evening. There was a problem with one jump hill in that if I didn't turn in time after the landing I would wind up in the middle of Highway 50 with the possibility of being run over by a passing car. I still remember Father reasoning me out of using that jump hill and finding a better location. Father could be as realistic as I could be recalcitrant, and I moved the jumping hill. We were the only family for several miles in wintertime Zephyr Cove and there were no other kids nearby. My parents neither skied nor were interested in the outdoors, so necessity mandated that I learn to amuse myself. I practiced slalom, jumped and took long rambles in the snow covered hills above Zephyr Cove on my one pair of wooden skis with screwed in metal edges and front throw cable bindings. I learned to cope with and then cherish solitude in action on skis, and those times were among the happiest of my childhood. I was nearly paralyzed with excitement one Christmas morning to see a new pair of skis under the tree, wrapped except for the tails which revealed the tell-tale three grooves in the bottom that marked jumping skis, my first pair. Soon after, I acquired cross-country skis which I used for racing, tramping around the woods and skiing the mile to the one room school at Zephyr Point. Our teacher, Ruth Little, educated eight students in the first eight grades, a complicated task she managed with skill, grace, insight and a great deal of care. That same Christmas Mrs. Little gave me a subscription to Ski Magazine where I was able to read about the 1950 World Championships in Aspen and about the incomparable Italian Zeno Colo, who won two gold and one silver medal in those races and who in skillful deed and sinister appearance was to my young eyes the coolest human being who had ever put a ski on edge.

On winter nights in our Zephyr Cove house I played canasta and poker with my parents and cribbage and chess with my father, and we listened to all the popular radio shows of the time--Jack Benny, Horace Heidt, the Lone Ranger, the Shadow, Fibber McGee and Molly, George Burns and Gracie Allen and the news. We read the newspapers and listened to the news and were always aware of if not completely informed about the larger world. More than 50 years later when I saw the film "Good Night and Good Luck" about the legendary newscaster Edward R. Murrow, I remembered his newscasts and was stunned that the film absolutely nailed the dress, hair styles, body postures, voice inflections and obsession with and posing manner of smoking the ever present cigarette of my parents and their generation. (The film also nails the best hope and greatest danger of what at this 2016 writing is the failing experiment of American democracy.) But for the most part, in winter after school and skiing I read. The printed word was as much a gift to my young being as was skiing. By nature and circumstance my parents were not forthcoming about the stories of their lives, and so it was the stories in books by which I oriented and guided myself through and into the intricacies of a path in this world. A love of reading is invaluable to a young person. My parents, like all parents, can be easily faulted by the fault finders (including myself), but they abundantly provided me with the written word and skiing and the opportunity (and freedom) to do with them both what I could and world. Many parents then and now have done far worse with far more self-congratulation.

From the famous adventure stories of Jack London to the obscure ones of Monte Atwater (whose writing has been forgotten but who was a pioneering legend in American avalanche forecasting and control work who later became a friend and was among the best poker players I ever knew) to the Mike Hammer trash detective sleaze side of life stories of Mickey Spillane, I gained an appreciation and yearning for experiences of life beyond what I could see around me. I read Mark Twain and the magazines of the time--Life, Look, the Saturday Evening Post, Field&Stream, and comic books and comic strips, especially Li'l Abner which was unrivaled as comic American social commentary until the arrival of Doonesbury, Earle Stanley Gardner, Marco Polo, Montaigne and anything I could find on skiing, which wasn't much. Reading was as big a part of education and daily life as school, parents, friends and even skiing. At some point as a pre-teenager, the admiration and gratitude I felt for writers evolved into the idea that maybe I could do a little writing too. It was a big idea for a little boy, but it never went away.

To find meaning, refuge, direction and unending learning in both outdoor activity and bookish contemplation at the same time was a fine balance in a boy's life and, as it worked out, a man's.

My parents almost always drove me to the ski races and jumping competitions those first couple of years. Most events were within the Tahoe Basin, none of them more than a few miles outside in places like Sky Tavern near Reno, Sugar Bowl and Royal Gorge on Donner Pass, and Nebelhorn and Edelweiss on Echo Pass. On occasion the meets were two day events and we would spend the night, often in Tahoe City. The parents of the junior racers formed their own alliances, social groups and parties that were as enjoyable to them as the races were to the kids. By day we hurtled ourselves down mountains, leapt off ski jumps and raced our hearts out around cross-country ski tracks with everything we had, learning in those small first steps the essential lessons of competition and personal awareness that you can get and be better, there will always be someone better, there will always be someone worse, and "....the important thing was commitment, and I found in myself the ability to give everything, to lay the whole show on the line. In that ability is hidden happiness, and all men have it, lurking somewhere amidst neuroses, education, experience, belief and centered in the heart. Success, while certainly not unimportant, is a problematical (mathematical) afterthought."

Still, I took inordinate pride in whatever accomplishments I could manage, in my case doing well in skiing competitions. I displayed in my room the trophies, medals, cups and ribbons I won, and they shored up several storerooms of insecurities and perceived or real personal inadequacies I would not begin to deal with for decades. I have sometimes wondered whether or not I would have invested so much personal value and self-respect in those trophies and what they represented if my parents had not made such a big thing (a trip to a photographer's studio 60 miles away and the photo prominently displayed in the house) out of the first one I won. Thirty years later those trophies would become as instructive as had been the process of acquiring them when my 4th wife, piqued because I had gone to China on a climbing expedition, took them to the town dump and disposed of them.

Ski jumping was my favorite event. I don't remember the first jump or where it happened, but nothing matched the thrill of anticipation and uncertainty of moving down the inrun of a ski jump, building up enough speed to launch oneself weightlessly into the air. Speed, skill and size of the jump hill determined how far one flew, how long a skier defied gravity; but those few seconds of floating were beautiful beyond measure. The distance a jumper flew could be measured and the technical form he used could be judged, the two combined to determine who won and who was next in the competitions; but the transcendent sensation of self-controlled, nonmechanized flight could only be experienced and processed, never measured, judged, seen or, in the end, described. Those first jumps were not long--50 to 80 feet--but I spent many afternoons, usually alone, sometimes with friends, hiking up jump hills, putting on skis, sliding down the inrun and leaping into the sky, stopping and hiking back up with the skis over my shoulder, over and over and over until fading light forced me indoors. Ski jumping was never King in Sierra Nevada ski circles and with each year the time, effort and importance put into it diminished, but I always loved it.

Slalom was the easiest to practice. All one needed was a snow covered hill, a few willows to use as slalom gates, and a couple of hours to side step up and down until the snow was in good enough shape to set a course. Then you skied down the course and hiked back up and skied the course again and hiked back up and skied the course and hiked back up, again and again and again. And you did it alone. There were plenty of suitable slopes near all the houses we lived in at Tahoe, and circumstances dictated that I ran slalom by myself far more than I ever did with other skiers, a practice I continued, not surprisingly, to the end of ski racing at the age of 27. Self-taught behavior, like so many habits of mind acquired in childhood, proved to serve me and my ski racing both well and ill, but I neither recognized nor understood its larger limitations until long after racing was done. Nature, evolution and the exacting anxieties of survival made primitive man an interdependent tribal creature. Independence from the tribe is a dangerous but not always fatal fantasy, but whether solitude is a choice or a circumstance the education that grows from it instills a trust between student and teacher that is not always found in more traditional educational dynamics. Learning on one's own has always taken place and always will; but the solitary, the self-taught and the serious dreamer at some level neglect the goals, rationale, support and limitations of the established community, as the solitary is neglected by establishment, even in the small, esoteric tribe of skiers.

In the course of thousands of runs down and hikes back up little slalom courses on the hills around Lake Tahoe I learned my lessons of skiing from the tools at hand. The first lesson was obvious to me early on at a level requiring no thought but which I recognized years later as articulated by Albert Camus in his essay on Sisyphus: "...Sisyphus is the absurd hero. He is, as much through his passions as through his torture. His scorn of the gods, his hatred of death, and his passion for life won him that unspeakable penalty in which the whole being is exerted toward accomplishing nothing. This is the price that must be paid for the passions of this earth....I leave Sisyphus at the foot of the mountain! One always finds one's burden again. But Sisyphus teaches the higher fidelity that negates the gods and raises rocks. He too concludes that all is well. This universe henceforth without a master seems to him neither sterile nor futile. Each atom of that stone, each mineral flake of that night filled mountain, in itself forms a world. The struggle itself toward the heights is enough to fill a man's heart. One must imagine Sisyphus happy."

I was a happy boy.

Chapter II
TRAVEL LESSONS

"The world is a book, and those who do not travel read only a page."
Saint Augustine

"I shall be telling this with a sigh somewhere ages and ages hence: Two roads diverged in a woods, and I--I took the one less traveled by, and that has made all the difference."
Robert Frost

"It is not down in any map; true places never are."
Herman Melville

There's no place like home but it doesn't follow inevitably that home is static ground. Home is where the heart is, and the searching, restless heart of a traveler is at home in the journey. Ski racing provided both motivation and mechanism for my first travel experiences out of the immediate Tahoe/Reno area, journeys without parents. The first in 1953 to the Junior National Championships in Brighton, Utah, involved my first plane ride from Reno to Salt Lake City. I traveled with Cathy Zimmerman, one year my senior who was the best young female skier in Reno. Cathy was my ski racing sister and a life long friend. My lovely, loving aunt Esther, my father's half-sister, lived in Provo and she and her husband C.B. picked us up in Salt Lake and drove us to Brighton in Big Cottonwood Canyon. Esther was one of my favorite relatives; she knitted me fine ski sweaters for several years and loved me with unremitting enthusiasm. I was always appreciated, cared for and safe in her presence.

My roommate at the Brighton Junior Nationals was Royal Robbins, a southern California ski racer three years older. I liked Royal and enjoyed his company and skiing with him, but our paths crossed infrequently after that until more than 15 years later when we met up again and Royal became a pivotal figure in my life. Dave McCoy, the founder and owner of Mammoth Mountain ski Area, was our coach for the Far West Ski Association. He also became a life long friend. More than 50 years later I do not know that I've ever met a more genuinely good and decent human being than Dave. I am one of many people who consider Dave to be an inspiration and guidepost in their lives. We had to bootpack the race courses in the soft, Utah powder and it was arduous work. Some of the racers skipped this communal chore and they were criticized by many of the racers who did show up. I was struck at the time that Dave neither criticized nor judged those who weren't there to pack, but he made sure the Far West skiers were present. Something about that informed and endeared Dave and his gap-toothed, square-jawed, no-nonsense smile to a 14 year old boy from Reno.

For the first time I was in the presence of dozens of kids and their coaches and, in some cases, their parents from all over the country. I saw that regional differences in people were real, sometimes clear, often subtle, always interesting. Like the Barkers of Clayton, the young ski racers of eastern America and the Rockies of Colorado and host state of Utah were exotic, fascinating and quite different in several ways from the skiers of California and Nevada. Grass grown in different soils naturally contains the elements of the particular soil which nurtures it, but in the end it is still grass. In broad generalities, my first impressions were that the eastern skiers dressed better and more fashionably and were more formal and reserved than we were around Reno; the Rocky Mountain skiers were more rustic and country cowboy like, and they were as a group the best skiers; and the Mormons of Utah were certainly aloof and insular compared to the raucous, irreverent Reno racers I knew best; while the northwest skiers seemed sophisticated and cosmopolitan beyond their years. First impressions.

Those impressions were neither complete nor entirely accurate, but they were another inoculation against the tendency to parochialism, the curse of every culture and the false refuge of......the parochial. More than 50 years after those races in Brighton, I still see, chat with and enjoy the company of one of the racers met there: Marvin Melville, a Utah Mormon boy, two time Olympic skier, political and social conservative and I have quite different religious beliefs, social values and circles of friends; but I have a great deal of respect and admiration for Marvin and his life and both trust his character and enjoy his company. A competitor to the core, Marvin still remembers and is rankled that Mel Hoagland from Aspen beat him for the slalom title in those races.

Just before leaving for Brighton a Reno radio station was interviewing Cathy and me about our forthcoming journey. We were in the radio station, 14 and 15 years old and very excited to be on the radio, when our interview was interrupted by the announcement that Joseph Stalin had died. In my young mind Stalin was a bad man and an enemy of America, both premises which later education and maturity confirmed, and his death is remembered and mentioned here to emphasize that even as a boy I felt and realized a connection to, a curiosity about, and a part in the larger world outside my teen-age friends, outside Reno, outside the tribe of skiing. Not all of my contemporaries felt that way. Not all of my contemporaries feel that way today, preferring the insular to the open as attitude and approach to life's challenges, opportunities and possibilities. Ten years after my first junior nationals I was rooming with one of America's finest ski racers at a training camp. This man, a life-long friend who after ski racing became a successful and wealthy businessman and I were talking in our room one night after training about the books I was reading. I happened to have a book of the writings of John Donne and William Blake. I read him some pieces from each of those writers, including, I remember, Donne's Meditation XVII, Devotions upon Emergent Occasions:

"No man is an island entire of itself; every man
is a piece of the continent, a part of the main;
if a clod be washed away by the sea, Europe
is the less, as well as if a promontory were, as
well as any manner of thy friends or of thine
own were; any man's death diminishes me,
because I am involved in mankind.
And therefore never send to know for whom
the bell tolls; it tolls for thee."

And this from Blake's "Auguries of Innocence:"

"To see a World in a Grain of Sand
And a Heaven in a Wild Flower,
Hold Infinity in the palm of your hand
And Eternity in an hour."

I still remember my friend's response to these and other literary bon mots which seemed to me to contain significant portent, value and meaning for our lives, for all human life. "I just don't see how that stuff is going to help my life, or even what it has to do with me." He was not kidding, disparaging or arguing; he was honestly, cheerfully and without judgment pointing out that a grain of sand is just a grain of sand and that the bell really doesn't toll for him and damn well isn't going to until it does and for him it won't matter by then. He had things to do, worlds to conquer, dragons to slay, goals to reach, and the work of people like John Donne and William Blake were of no use to him. He was as amused as he was puzzled by the time I spent reading such things, and, in truth, I was as amused as I was puzzled by his focus on the practical at the expense of larger, grander, more ethereal and literary issues.

Ski racing was the slice of life by which I most clearly began to see and experience one of humanity's great conundrums: we are all the same, and no two of us are even remotely alike.

Physically, all children grow up at roughly the same rate, regardless of what their biological or other parents do or do not do. Mentally, emotionally and spiritually, they evolve along different trajectories at wildly different velocities. Social norms for adults and sub-adults are not sacred, impermeable nor as compassionately wholesome as adherents of the status-quo would prefer to believe. This was especially so in 1950s repressively bland Eisenhower era America in which I passed through adolescence.

In June of 1956 I graduated from Reno High School. In September of that year I enrolled at the University of Nevada in Reno to study journalism and English. The following month I turned 18 and broke up with my longtime steady girlfriend. I was both freed and saddened by the split and was behaving with predictable abandon. My primary interests were parties, ski racing, girls, literature, jazz and driving automobiles at high rates of speed, not necessarily in that order. I was more bookish than many, more athletic than most, but in many ways not untypical of my contemporaries. It was a great time of life despite the normal difficulties and insecurities of being rebellious and angry in an insipid era of saccharine shallowness and sterile hypocrisy that the '60s would none too soon strip naked. I was as joyfully full of life (and myself) as I could be. I was well into adulthood before recognizing and being able to name in myself the murderous rage running just beneath the surface of my entire generation. One need not apologize for nor rationalize the inherent contradictions, confusions and sadness of a joyous life of rage. One incident from that time is indicative and, as it proved, consequential:

One early December 1956 weekday night me and my long time best buddy W--- were drinking beers in the Little Waldorf, the favorite bar for Nevada students. Usually we drank only on weekends, but for reasons since forgotten we were out on a school night. Possibly, one of us was feeling depressed (we called it 'being down'), alienated or insecure and had enticed the other out for beer and companionship. This lapse of teen-age social/drinking protocol coincided with a fire in one of the campus sorority houses that night. As a result, several temporarily homeless sorority girls were also drinking beer in the Little Wal'. Two of them, A--- and N---, were casual friends from skiing; but neither W--- nor I had ever dated or had any conversations that went deeper than a polite flirtation with either of them. Still, intentions are crucial, and there is no purity of heart or innocence in fleeting flirtation. The four of us wound up in W---'s Chevy sedan parked in one of Reno's dark, secluded parking spot refuges, W--- and N--- in the front seat, me and A--- in the back. Soon we were all 'making out,' kissing, fondling and completely wrapped up in the unrivaled pleasure of sexual foreplay. Literally before we knew it, A--- and I were 'going all the way.' We had sex. We fucked. Waaaahoooooo!!! We fucked quietly, of course. We were not alone, and sex was taboo in that conservative 1950's

Nevada culture which hypocritically if civilly pretended that its legalization of gambling, 24 hour a day drinking, prostitution, quick and easy divorce and quicker and easier marriage was not the foundation of its economy and, therefore, its social values. Sex never needs help to find its own way, but it is true that the taboo of sex added to its allure. It wasn't talked about, and in 1950s America what you pretended you didn't do was far more important (and noted) than what you did. Pretense overlay reality as the standard of social norms in my society. Thus, personal dishonesty was built into the fabric of growing up by an impossible to live by but transparent social fabrication. Making sex forbidden fruit is, ultimately, fruitless. After that night A--- and I pretended to each other and to the world that nothing had happened. In January I left school for the winter in order to train for ski racing in Colorado. I thought of A--- that winter and intended to ask her out for a date when I returned to Reno in the spring. I liked and wanted to get to know her. But when the racing season ended and I returned to town, I learned she had quit school to marry her high school sweetheart. She had left Reno. I remember some disappointment. Women were strange and mysterious creatures. Who could tell what they might do next?

In January 1957 I quit college after one semester and moved to Aspen to train and ski race. I shared a room in a private home with two other racers, Ron Funk and Tony Perry.

Ron, five years my senior, raised by his grandmother in Oregon after his parents divorced, had already been married, sired a daughter and divorced. He was intense, curious, opinionated, funny and with a bright intelligence that was and remained to the end of his life more than 50 years later seriously skewed by a twisted, misogynist's cynicism toward traditional family values and American culture in general. (He explained the rationale behind his first divorce thus: "She squeezed the toothpaste tube in the middle.") He was a wiry athlete with a round head (earning him the sobriquet "Melonhead") and a facial resemblance to the actor Marlon Brando. He was a fierce competitor who pushed the limits of his abilities at all times. Sometimes he pushed beyond those limits and as a consequence suffered more injuries than most of his peers of a lifestyle in which few escaped injury. Like blizzards, icy roads, dangerous race courses and phony, pretentious people such injuries were accepted as normal if disagreeable challenges. Ron became my first close friend who lived by and embraced the free-spirited, open-minded values that our culture terms "counter-culture." His life-long friendship had a huge influence on many aspects of my life.

Tony, a year older than me, was also a child of divorced parents, his father a renowned, crusty, successful hotelier in Stowe, Vermont. A Vermonter who went to a private high school in Colorado, Tony was also taking a semester out of university (Denver) studies to ski race. He was smart, funny and free-spirited, though economic success in life held a higher priority and far more allure for Tony than it did for me or Ron. The previous year I swung into the top bunk in our dorm room in Sun Valley, where we were rooming together at a ski race, just as Tony leaned over to take off his shoes before bed. My knee accidentally caught him flush in the nose, breaking it badly and moving it to one side of his face, and we had to spend part of that night in the hospital. So we were well connected before the winter in Aspen, and Tony and I also became life-long friends. Once we went more than 20 years without seeing each other and when we met up in Aspen in the early 1990s and started talking we were both struck by the ease with which we communicated, as if we had taken up a conversation in mid-sentence from a couple of decades before.

It was a good winter in Aspen, my last year as a teen-ager, sharing a room with friends. By day we skied and trained. By night we socialized and partied. Mostly we talked--about everything, with everybody, and it was a less formal and far more useful education for a 18 year old than I would have gotten in the classrooms of the University of Nevada. Though I did not know it and would not know of it for 38 years, while I was living in Aspen with my two friends and skiing every day and living a life that many would consider carefree and simple my first child was gestating in his mother's womb as a consequence of our backseat encounter in early December.

It was a strange and mysterious world, full of pitfalls and inexpressible beauty. At 18 I understood less of its traps and its splendor than I would in later years, but there is much to recommended the raw, direct experience of life at that age. As a ski racer the winter of 1957 was deeply beneficial. I matured as a skier, learned much about technique and training and attitude, became enamored in ways I would not recognize for a few years of the lifestyle we knew in Aspen and, most important, realized that there were many people who shared my love for skiing and free form life that could not embrace and, at best, tolerated authority and social "norms."

BOOK FOUR

Chapter I
THE SORTING OUT

"Almost everyone has a predominant inclination, to which his other desires and affections submit, and which governs him, though with perhaps some intervals, through the whole course of his life."
David Hume

Fill your bowl to the brim and it will spill. Keep sharpening your knife and it will blunt. Chase after money and security and your heart will never unclench. Care about people's approval and you will be their prisoner. Do your work, then step back. The only path to serenity.
Tao-te-ching

Depending on how deep you sink or dive into it, discouragement can be a great teacher and ally. If you go too deep you may never surface and will live a dull-edged life with a clenched heart and a prisoner's mind. If you make it back to the surface and swim to shore and dry out on the beach of a higher perspective, you might see that discouragement is another of life's incessant hard questions that can only be answered by the path of your life. By the summer of 1957 I was discouraged with my ski racing and decided that I would quit racing and only ski for recreation, return to school, study hard, immerse myself in the university social scene including fraternity life, party, chase girls, listen to good music, read good books and in general become a good citizen and participating member of the American social order in ways that I had previously avoided. Ski racing, it seemed, was no longer bringing me deep satisfaction, despite the many good times and memories and people associated with it. That season left me with a sense of frustration and sometimes humiliation and without a sense of direction. Besides, what I liked most about skiing was being outside in the snow and clean air in beautiful mountain scenery immersed in a really enjoyable activity and, usually, in the company of like-minded and-spirited friends. I didn't need to compete to have that. Right?

In that time skiing was a cherished part of healthy recreation for a small segment of Reno's mainstream social order. For reasons which now escape me some part of my 18 year old personality sought that order's approval, and during the next few years I gave a mighty effort to gain it. Fortunately, my instincts sabotaged every endeavor to live a traditional life of conventional values in the supporting company of mainstream people. The conformist values of America embodied at the time in the bland if brutal conservative imperialism of Dwight Eisenhower and the deceptive, morally vicious personal ambitions of Richard Nixon, respectively President and Vice-President of the United States, simply didn't feel right to me. It would be several years before I gained the skills and awareness to understand and articulate the danger and degradation conventional America offered its citizens under the canon of 'standard of living.' Like every mammal in the 200 million year history of Mammalia and before that in its reptile ancestors, I had a perfectly sound and continuously evolving instinctive system to warn me of the presence and approach of danger. But it's hard to heed those instincts when it's so easy to let them be overridden by the pat on the back of approval from contemporaries who rightfully expect a counter-instinctive pat of approval in return. Flinching at the former and not reciprocating the latter are threatening to every social order in history, and neither are rewarded or ignored by that order. Every path in life exacts its price, bestows its pleasures and rewards, and is filled with obstacles, riddles, burdens and obscure sidetracks. Each path is lined with comrades, friends, enemies and critics, all of whom are on their own paths and for whom you might be a comrade, friend, enemy, critic, pleasure or burden, perhaps all of them at different times and stages of the journey.

In the long run we are all on the same path, though that is neither obvious nor acceptable to an 18 year old boy, nor does this become clear to all too many for all their lives.

That summer of 1957 I enrolled in summer school at the university. I studied hard and particularly enjoyed a music appreciation course in which I learned that Benny Goodman, one of my heroes of jazz, also played classical music. This was revelation to my badly informed mind, and I listened to Goodman play classical music with new appreciation. If it was good enough for Benny it was good enough for me. I began listening to classical music with the same interest as jazz, and a bit more light entered the vast darkness of my ignorance. I partied hard on weekends, took hikes in the nearby Sierra Nevada and made a few trips to San Francisco to listen to jazz and hang out in coffee houses and bars that were as different from the bars of Reno as, say, the Nevada desert was from the San Francisco bay. Though we were all under the legal drinking age of 21 we were seldom refused a drink in either state, and we drank as hard as my parents and their friends. There was a freedom of conversation, an open attitude, a sense of excitement and importance to the feel of the bars and music and coffee houses and book stores and streets of San Francisco that was absent in Reno. I was drawn to and inspired by that freedom and was always a little discontented upon returning to Reno. Whether discontent grows from or grows into an awareness of differences is less important than the awareness itself. The basis of those differences was in the opening of the mind to different ideas, stepping outside the parochial, familiar template. San Francisco bookstores had a different selection than could be found in Reno. My favorite was City Lights on Columbus Avenue. Black, yellow, tan and white skinned people sat in the same bars and restaurants in San Francisco, while Reno was segregated until 1962 when U.S Attorney General Bobby Kennedy became the first person in his job to enforce the interstate commerce laws and force the casinos to desegregate. Gay people in San Francisco were part of the culture while in Reno gay people were shunned, denigrated, sent scurrying to the closet and beaten up in back alleys.

By mid-June that year I had earned a few extra pounds of beer fat belly and in response got into the practice of taking long runs in the dusty, hot, sagebrush hills around Reno. I had always trained for ski racing, starting in September or October, but strangely enough since I wasn't going to ski race again that summer I began training at a much higher level of intensity and duration than I ever had before. Perhaps it was only vanity training, but after a few weeks I felt really good after workouts, maybe because I was training for the sake of keeping care of my body and not for better results in a ski race. Conceivably it was simply that my body craved intense exercise. Whatever the reason or reasons for my newborn discipline, I loved it and soon found a group of running buddies, some of them boxers at the University, and rarely missed a day of running and pumping iron. Long runs in Nevada summer heat will make a body sweat and lose weight, but one of those boxers, Sam Macias, turned me on to a neat trick to accelerate the process--wearing a rubber shirt under the sweatshirt on a hot Nevada day will cause the driest of bodies to expel the excess liquid within, a fine if not pain or effortless weight loss/physical fitness program.

I worked out, partied on weekends, studied, read books, thought about and consciously began to observe life and the world as more than what I could make, get or understand of them. Something began to change for me and the slow process of maturity perceptibly accelerated. The lazy comforts of social norms were more alluring than usual and it was the closest I ever came to fully embracing the cultural/social values and goals of my time and society. It took a couple of years before the embrace broke off, but for a time I was on the mainstream path of college education leading to a job in the marketplace, social status, acceptance by my peers, a mortgage and life in Reno and who knows what else?

And that summer my mother--in her early 40s, not in good health, a heavy drinker and smoker, who had lost one child just after birth and legally aborted another because of medical problems and had been told she could never have another child--announced that she was pregnant. More, she was determined to have the child. Father, who was as surprised as me and a great deal more troubled by it, immediately if a few months too late got a vasectomy and limped around for a few days before he healed. That summer I was 18 years old, living with mom and dad and mom was pregnant with my only sibling, a move in a larger strategy of war my parents had carried on as a continuation of World War II. Since I was nearly out of the home, father had bought a small plot of land with a cabin in the desert near Silver Springs east of Carson City where he intended to retire and grow cantaloupes and watch sunsets in solitude. Mom, a social animal whose cocktail gatherings with her friends were crucial to her happiness or at least to coping with her unhappiness, wasn't about to give them up for solitude, sunsets and cantaloupes. Nor was she going to stay in Reno on her own and give up the pleasures of the war, the securities of her husband's job and the only life she could imagine. Getting pregnant and obligating my good and responsible father to the raising of another child was Mom's ticket to stability and an unchanging view. In September my own first son was born, four months before my only brother, but I was not to know of his existence for nearly 40 years.

That fall Governor Orval Faubus in Arkansas and Sputnik in space helped the thoughtful think about the fault lines of America's racism and about the Cold War between Russia and America. My father was general manager of the New China Club, at that time Reno's only casino that allowed black people in its doors. When I was a small boy we had lived as the only white family on the Paiute Reservation at Pyramid Lake, so awareness of racism was part of my family in ways it was not for most of Reno's predominately white society. The previous year I had turned 18 and was required to register for the draft. Racism and war were things we discussed in our home, and early on I learned to be skeptical of any argument justifying either. Since racism and war are integral to the history, economy, politics and cultural values of America, I also learned to be skeptical of the nationalism, patriotism and boosterism endemic to American society which conveniently forgets that the nation was built on the bedrock of the slavery of blacks and the genocide of Indians and that it had dropped two atomic bombs on Japanese cities filled mostly with women and children. In the long view, those bombs did as much damage to the American psyche as they did to the cities and citizens of Hiroshima and Nagasaki. Even at 18 my thoughts and feelings about my country were beginning to run counter to its culture, though it would be a few years before that was clear enough for me to put into words.

That fall I continued at the University as a journalism major with a full load of courses More than 40 years later I wrote a column about the best of what I learned that year in the journalism department:

"Journalists are often denounced for lacking "objectivity" in their work. Such accusations, in my opinion, are more often than not without merit, even though they are true. As a journalism student at the University of Nevada in the 1950s I don't remember objectivity being discussed specifically as a tool of the second oldest profession, though the concept was understood to be a sacred tenet of the trade. How could one not be objective about who, what, where, when, why and how? Objectivity was never actually defined (how could it be?), but it seemed to encompass such concepts as fairness, truth, balance, presenting all sides of an issue, checking facts with a critical and skeptical mind and to never, ever accept without question and independent research the 'official' (usually press release) version of anything given out by the political, corporate, military, bureaucratic and even personal front men we referred to as flacks but which now have other titles, both pretentious and colloquial, including press secretary, public relations officer, spokesman and spin doctor. In my opinion, it is on this latter point that American journalism deserves bountiful criticism, not for lacking objectivity.

"This was useful information, objectivity as a reliable ideal, a goal. Fortunately, our journalism professors, A.L. Higginbotham and Keiste Janulis, were men of the real world of gradation and doubt and organic, unending questioning, not fundamentalists with obdurate answers to limited questions, though "Higgie" could be evangelical when it came to the importance and value of good journalism and a free press to a free society. In every class (especially Janulis'), without making it an issue, it was made clear that pure journalistic objectivity was as unreal as such imaginative concepts as virgin birth, Santa Claus and the more recent phantasm of compassionate conservatism. Journalism, like everything it reported, was not black or white, good or evil, with us or against us, but, rather, an on going dialogue, discovery and evolving perspective as reported by flesh and blood and all too subjective human beings. Objectivity, it seemed, was all too subjective. How could it not be? A hundred journalists will have a hundred different definitions of objectivity. In recognition of this dilemma, the Society of Professional Journalists dropped "objectivity" from its ethics code in 1996.

"Janulis had worked as an AP reporter and traveled the world and viewed the affairs and machinations of man with a bemused skepticism befitting a professional journalist. He was Lithuanian, and had been news editor of the Baltic Times in Estonia, covered World War II for the Chicago Tribune, earned a master's degree in journalism from Columbia University, and had studied German and Russian propaganda at the University of Lithuania. He knew that the world was filled with nuance and danger and that neither safety nor truth could be found in absolutes. Janulis' perspective appealed to me in part because it was so human. That is, ethically he was a professional, not a proselytizer. Journalism was a profession practiced by humans, and anyone who expects objectivity from humans is being neither objective nor attentive.

"I have always been thankful that Higgie and Jan were my teachers in that formative time.

"In one course our textbook was a well known national weekly news magazine. We were primarily print media students and we read the magazine cover to cover each week, examining every photo, advertisement, story, review, editorial and letter to the editor. It was considered the standard of good journalism at that time, but we learned that pure objectivity about even who, what, where, when, why, and how was easier said than done. We learned to look for what was left out of a story and we talked about how the story could be written differently with the same set of facts. We compared letters to the editor with the previous stories that inspired them, and discussed letters we might write concerning the same stories. We looked for the particular bias and perspective (the angle) that produced the story. Years later a friend who wrote for this magazine told me about quitting after covering the story of the sinking of the U.S. nuclear submarine Thresher in 1963. He interviewed dozens of family members of the 129 men who died in the accident 200 miles off Cape Cod. Many of them reported that their dead loved ones had anticipated such a failure on what was reputed to be the most advanced submarine ever built and had complained their safety was compromised. The magazine refused to include these pertinent remarks in the article because they reflected badly on the U.S. military, not a popular perspective in those Cold War days. While there may be some national security justifications for such editing, it is neither complete nor objective (whatever that means) journalism, but it was an insider's illustration of the particular biases and perspectives we studied in school.

"And, of course, even then, in those days of the decent if bland, squeaky clean Eisenhower and 99.9 percent pure Ivory soap and calling for Philip Morris, we noted and looked for correlations between advertising and the editorial and news content of a publication. Then, as now, they were easy to find.

"In addition to the purely human obstacles to objectivity in journalism, there are economic ones. Journalism, too, is a business. This is not to condone or excoriate the excesses and limitations of journalism, but only to recognize them for what they are and what they are not.

"The only objectivity is outside the purview of journalism as we know it, that which includes everyone and everything. Jim Harrison said it best: "... reality is an aggregate of the perceptions of all creatures, not just ourselves.""

Because I had already taken most of the journalism classes and because it seemed to me that the writing I wanted to do was more literary than reportage I changed my major to English with journalism as a minor the next year. I have always been grateful for those first, faltering insights into the aggregate of perceptions that compose reality. Among the most useful lessons of my university education are that life is nuance and shades of gray and the full rainbow spectrum of bright and muted colors, not black and white, fundamentalist or absolute.

By October the university ski team was training several afternoons a week--running, lifting weights, playing soccer, doing the ubiquitous calisthenics and torturous stretching exercises and taking weekend hikes in the Sierra. I joined them for the workout and the camaraderie, I told myself. Several friends were on the ski team, including Harry Ericson, Dave Pruett, Don Cronin, Jack Bosta, Tom Nicora, Mary Ann Tonini and Fran Beer and they, along with friend and University Ski Team coach Chelton Leonard, encouraged me to think about racing for the University for fun, for the pleasure of racing, for the team, for the camaraderie, for the hell of it, and to quit being so damn serious about something so inconsequential as sliding down a snow covered hill on a pair of turned up sticks. Skiing was fun. What other possible significance could it have? Why not have some fun skiing for the University with friends so long as you're in school anyway? Why not?

Why not?

So, I returned to ski racing that winter. Just for fun. And it was fun. It was also the only time I ever attended both the fall and winter semesters (as well as summer school) the same year.

Chapter II
CONFORMITY

"Conformity is the jailer of freedom and the enemy of growth."
John F. Kennedy

For the next three years I did my best to buy into the American dream. I tried as hard as I knew how, I tried I tried I tried to become a good, vibrant, intelligent, true-believing and conforming participant in the dominant cultural and societal mores, values and goals of my country and time. Ultimately, I could never succeed in this endeavor. It was a futile quest, though it would be years before I could understand and verbalize the practical wisdom of Theodore Roszak's contention that "alienation is the passport to contemporary relevance" and that conformity is irrelevant if sometimes comfortable and far, far more dangerous and destructive than the insecurities of individual alienation. But, first, I tried.

I involved myself in several aspects of university life--social, chemical, fraternal, sexual, literary and athletic. I had friends close and casual, each of us growing along different trajectories and velocities. The only drug I was familiar with was alcohol, usually beer, sometimes wine, seldom any of the harder varieties of America's drug of choice. Sigma Nu took me in and for a year I was a devoted fraternity man/boy. I still consider the Sigma Nu initiation/hell week to be one of the stupidest ordeals I have ever inflicted on myself. A few years later, long after I had ceased any participation in fraternity life, I was bemused that my mother became President of the Sigma Nu Mother's Club. In popular cultural myth the 60s were the decade of sexual liberation, but it was my experience that the 50s certainly gave it a head (sic) of steam to get it going. I wrote a short story for the University literary magazine Brushfire and began spending time with the arts and literary people of the University and was far more intellectually and emotionally comfortable with them than with the machojocks of the athletic department, though I trained with the ski team and sometimes with members of the boxing team and spent as much time as anyone around the athletic department.

It was an enjoyable, satisfying year at the University and, at least on the surface, an indication that I was headed for a very different life than the one I wound up living. I had the best season ever as a ski racer, both for the University and in larger competitions, including a 5th in the National Championships and winning the Sun Valley Open slalom against a strong field. By spring my confidence in skiing and in my self had recovered and made stronger by slogging through the previous year's discouragement, disappointments and frustrations. The slog was a good lesson that served me well in later years.

The same day (January 12, 1958) I won the Sun Valley Open slalom my mother gave birth to my brother, Louis Crawford at St. Mary's Hospital in Reno. In one of my scrapbooks I have a telegram mom sent to her sister-in-law Esther, illustrating her knowledge of Bill Haley's music as well as her sense of humor: "Shake, rattle and roll, Louis Crawford came out of his hidey hole." Mom and Dad were ill-prepared for the rigors of a new baby and I, of course, was clueless. Louis was born with a hernia and in 1958 hernias were not repaired on babies until they were several months old. Louis was sent home with a truss to hold his hernia in until he was big enough to risk surgery. Home was a small two bedroom apartment in a quiet neighborhood on Jones Street by the Truckee River. Mom was only a year or two away from being completely incapacitated by emphysema brought on by her twenty year smoking habit of three packs a day, exacerbated by poor diet, no exercise and alcoholism. Dad was only seven years from being committed to a VA hospital in Salt Lake for a nervous/mental breakdown brought on by trying to cope with Mom and Louis and life and the onset of a neurological disorder that he picked up on Guam during World War II. (See "Island of the Color Blind" by Oliver Sachs.) I was 19 years old and trying to ski race and go to college, and I had no idea that Mom's smoking would kill her or that alcoholism was a disease we were all prone to or that Dad was slowly coming undone. I did know that nearly every night Louis' truss would loosen while he slept and his hernia would come out and that Louis would shriek with pain and Mom and Dad would get up and push his hernia back in and comfort him and try to get him to sleep again. Sometimes Louis would go back to sleep and other times the pain was too great and he would cry for hours. It was excruciating for Louis and exhausting for everyone. One night when Louis was less than two months old and had been crying in pain for hours, Dad woke me and sent me to the nearest liquor store to buy some brandy. I did as he asked and came home with a pint of cheap brandy. With an eye dropper we dripped drops of brandy into Louis' screaming mouth as he lay on his back gasping for breath in agony. I don't remember how many drops it took or how long, but eventually Louis' eyes clouded, rolled back and closed and soon he went to sleep.

And then we all went to sleep.

And the next night when Louis' hernia came out and he began screaming the eye dropper and brandy also came out.

And the next night.

And the next.

And the next.

I don't remember how old Louis was before his hernia was repaired or how long after that before he could sleep through a night without unbearable pain, but it was several years before it occurred to me that dripping brandy into the body of a baby was a questionable practice with long-term consequences, especially a body with alcoholism rampant on both sides of its genetic code.

What were we thinking?

Sleep.

Brother Louis had a brutal beginning to life and he never had a chance at a normal, decent childhood, but like so many aspects of life what is crystal clear in hindsight was neither evident nor even considered in the interrupted sleep present moment of the Dorworth family in the middle of 1958 nights on Jones Street in Reno.

Alcohol was an integral part of the daily life of my family and the families of nearly everyone we knew. Most states do not have Nevada's 24 hour a day drinking laws, and, so far as I know, most families do not put their crying babies to sleep with brandy; but Nevada's laws and Louis' hernia medicine were (and are) only extreme instances of the dominant if largely unacknowledged cultural mores of America. Alcohol dulls pain and allows one to sleep until the root causes of that pain--hernia in the physical body, double-bind in the mind, sickness in the soul--are addressed, but there are consequences, always consequences.

Ski racing that winter was really enjoyable. I reveled in the racing, the team, the camaraderie, skiers I met from other teams for whom skiing was a different matter than it was for me. I kept telling myself it was only for fun at the same time I was both aware of the difference and appreciative of (some of) its import. Part of the pleasure was that I had some good results. Competition is a great game for the winners.

I dated frequently but had no girl friend, though late that spring I dated one girl, Farol, more than anyone else. Farol was an identical twin and we had gone to high school together. A year older than me, Farol was as entranced by the freedoms I allowed myself as I was attracted to her proper, conservative standards. We were having a good time together and were not 'serious' about our relationship. That, at least, is how I viewed it and believed and still believe she viewed it. Nevertheless, after the appropriate time of just making out and going home filled with frustration and sexual longing, we sometimes parked in some dark corner of western Nevada and made love in the back seat of my Chevy Bel-Air. The glories and pleasures of sex need no explanation, and loving the sex without loving the girl till death do us part delineated the relationship without diminishing the sex. Or so it seemed to me.

Still, who knows what might have happened if I hadn't gone to Chile that summer?

The previous winter's ski racing had been successful enough that I was encouraged to make a bid for the upcoming 1960 Olympic team. The Olympics were to be in nearby Squaw Valley and I determined that in order to prepare for the tryouts I would spend the summer training on the southern hemisphere snows of Chile. My aunt, Llewellyn Gross, helped me with finances and I was able to spend nearly three months training in what became my favorite country next to my own. Most of the skiing time was spent in Portillo, the oldest destination ski resort in South America which in 1958 consisted of one 125 room hotel by Laguna del Inca and a single chair lift high in the Andes near the Argentine border, accessible only via a cog railway.

The trip inspired what became a lifelong practice (sometimes interrupted for long periods, other times daily) of keeping journals. Leaving the United States for the first time was momentous for a 19 year old, and I knew I wanted to record what I could of the time, its events, the thoughts that arose and the lessons learned. That is when writing really began for me, when I first if dimly became aware that while epic journeys are momentous so is each day, every hour, each moment. Live them as you must, understand them as you can, record them if you will. Though I'd written since before I was a teenager and knew I wanted to write, it was the journals that gave it discipline, form and a place to grow. From that time on I've written something most days of my life--journal, journalism, essay, fiction, commentary, column, letters and book reviews, even poetry and a few songs. Good writing is composed more of discipline and practice than of inspiration, just like skiing, just like anything a human would do proficiently. Discipline is a great friend, a loyal servant, a poor master. If discipline is a tool it will help you build a palace in which to live; if it is a prison, it will keep you in a cell in which to die. I made friends with discipline, but I have come to know others who have not.

Chapter III
CHILE

*"About me, nothing worse they will tell you, my love, than what
I told you."*
Pablo Neruda

"Write what should not be forgotten."
Isabel Allende

The first entry on the first page of what became thousands
of pages of journals in the life of a writer was dated June 15,
though the year (1958) was not included. I had decided to write
what should not be forgotten many years before Isabel Allende,
who was but 15 when I first went to Chile, offered that advice
to writers and all people who wish to learn from the past rather
than forget it. It was a meager beginning, as shown by the first
entries, each in its entirety:

"June 15—Reno--Took Farol over to Gardnerville to get
David. Got along well with Farol and had a good time. Dave,
Farol and I had dinner with my folks. Went out with (x) Farol.

"June 16—Reno--Left Reno by bus for Oakland. Farol,
Buddy Sorenson and my folks saw us off. Bus ride was
miserable, as it stopped many times and the personnel was
discourteous. Howie met us at the depot and we ate and slept at
his house. Watched his movies of the FIS at Bad Gastein. They
made me anxious to ski.

"June 17--Spent the day in San Francisco. Saw Zooie Pruett
and her friend off at the "Leilani" party on the boat. Drank
champagne and tried to meet this girl. Her name was Barbara
but I had very poor luck. She was beautiful. Howie, Pruett's

family, and the Duggans saw us off at airport. Plane ride was good. We stopped in L.A. and I slept most of the way.

"June 18--Stopped in Guatemala which I liked and Managua which was too hot. We landed in Panama and stayed. The cab drivers and cargo boys screwed us but there was nothing we could do about it. Got a pension for $5 a night room and board. We showered, ate, and wandered around town. The slums are awful. The people speak Spanish, but many speak English. The weather is too hot. Dave knew enough Spanish to ask a student, studying in a park, where the whore house was. It was pretty funny. But we didn't go as it cost too much and the thought that the Negro whores might be 'dirty.'

"June 19--We rode the Panama buses all day for about 60 cents. We went to the canal and spent some time there. Took some pictures like typical tourists which we were. Had lunch in the U.S. commissary in Balboa. Then back to Panama City where we wandered around the city for the rest of the day. Wrote some letters that night and looked through the Panama Hilton hotel. It is tremendous. Much better than the pension we stayed in.

"June 20--Had our taxi driver, Ernest Soto, get us up at 5 a.m. so we could catch the plane at 6. He charged us $6.00, as before, to get to the airport. We ate breakfast there. Were served breakfast as soon as we got on the plane. Two American boys were on the plane with us. They were on their way to Peru to climb the highest mt. in the western world. One of them was sick the whole flight. There is no baggage compartment so the baggage is stored in the front of the passengers. Stopped in Cali, Columbia and Guayaquil, Equador. Landed in Lima and were met by a barrage of hotel agents. Cab driver took us again, but the Hotel Wilson was nice. Prices lower here. Ate in the best restaurant for $2.00. Looked the town over. Were followed by a shoeshine boy for two hours. Dave had a drink, I had a Ginger Ale at the hotel bar. Everybody tries to talk us "gringos" out of their money.

"June 21--Lima, Peru--Nancy was married in Reno today. I'm glad I wasn't there. I thought of her all day and often found myself regretting having given her up. Maybe I was wrong. I'll never know.

"We shopped and looked over the downtown area. I bought some Llama slippers for my folks and a bracelet for Farol. I don't think I'll give it to her, however. Dave bought a Llama rug for his parents, but I bet he keeps it. We went out to Ed Aimone's aunt's home. Mrs. Jackson and her husband Tom were wonderful. They took us on a tour of Lima and bought us lunch. The slums here are terrible, but San Isedro and other wealthy sections are beautiful.

"I liked Lima. I must have been thinking of Nancy or something because I got David and myself to the airport 24 hours early. A taxi driver pointed out our error and took us back to town. We were quite silly looking at midnight in an empty airport. We've finally got the taxi drivers. We tell them our price before we get in the cab."

The beginning of writing what should not be forgotten, the outline of a life marked by unrecognized privilege, unrequited longing, irreversible commitment to the journey and an incomprehensible inability to communicate an acceptable price before getting in the cab.

The (x) in the last sentence of the first journal entry of my life is code for fucking. As it turned out, (x) represented the last time we ever (x)ed. Like most of the sexual activity of that time, culture and age group our entire sexual life took place in the back seat of my car in the many dark, secret (so we thought) hideaways of the Nevada desert and the Sierra Nevada. It lasted a couple of months and then I went to Chile.

As the journal notes, I thought of her but was attached to neither her nor those thoughts. My notes do not reveal that I wrote her and I do not think I contacted her when I returned. We never talked about our sexual encounters. We just fucked. Since accepted social mores dictated that we weren't supposed to be doing what we were doing we got around the obvious conflict and social contradiction by never talking about it. Part of the daily life of 1950s America was the implicit understanding that if it wasn't discussed it didn't happen. At the time I couldn't even write in a private journal about something as joyous, enjoyable and natural as sex. Neither of us was a virgin when we first parked in those dark places around Reno, but the only thing I remember her ever saying about sex was after the first time when she said, "That's the first time I ever felt like a woman." I never forgot her saying that but I missed the significance of what she meant and concluded in my self-absorption that I must have been pretty good. Communication is the best antidote for the delusions of self-absorption and self-deception which are interchangeable, but the history of mankind is written in the code of missed communication.

There is some serious Puritanical (hypocritical) repression at work in a young man who feels it necessary to use (x) code in the privacy of his own journal to describe his own primal sex life. The trip to Chile was a first step in cutting through those blinders to self-knowledge and barriers to honest communication.

The other early journal entries reveal three streams of seeking that have guided and determined the path of much of my life...a desire to ski, an interest in women, and a curiosity about the world. My ex-girl friend Nancy was married the day we wandered around Lima and my heart and mind were heavy. My notes indicate a questioning of my decision to break up but the decision was not mine alone. That I wrote that it was, that I missed Farol's meaning in feeling like a woman, that a day after being sent off by Farol I was trying to meet a pretty, strange girl, that three days later only the price and a fear of infection kept me away from the Panama whores, and that a girl friend I had broken up with a year and a half earlier was still stirring my heart and swirling my mind reveals many things about a young man, including a shaky foundation for a healthy, happy, adult emotional life.

We arrived in Chile and made our way to Portillo. It was probably the last summer of innocence or, at least, naiveness.

Most of my notes for the time in Chile are filled with the technical and psychological aspects of ski racing, observations about a wide-range of new people in my experience and an expanding perspective on the lives we were leading. Mel Swensen, Phil Potvin, Jim Laird, Laurie Gibb, Rip McManus, Rosmarie Bogner, Willy Bogner, Fritz Wagnerberger, Vicho Vera, Victor Tagle, John Koppes, Misty Cumberledge and Ned Damon all became new friends whose lives would intertwine with my own for many years. I already knew Roger Crist, Fran Beer, Kalevi Hakkinen and the incomparable Olympic and World Champion skier Stein Eriksen from the States, and our lives, too, were to intertwine in unimaginable ways in future years. More than 50 years later Roger Crist and Rosmarie Bogner live in Ketchum, Idaho where I live and are still friends.

(An aside: Before she got out of college Fran Beer managed to break the hearts of two of my friends, Bob Autry and Warren Lerude, contributing to Warren's decision to drop out of college and join the Navy. I always liked Fran and enjoyed her company and was pleased to see her in Portillo, but it was always at least intuitively clear to me that she was a woman who could break your heart if you weren't careful.

After college I didn't see Fran for several years, though I heard she had married her high school sweetheart, who was reported to be a bright and good man and a Rhodes Scholar, and was raising a family in Palo Alto. In the winter of 1966 I ran into Fran at the Alpine Meadows ski area where she was spending a weekend and I was coaching a junior ski race team. I invited Fran Beer for a beer after skiing and we had an interesting visit. I told her I had heard her husband was a Rhodes Scholar and that she must be very pleased. She quickly disabused me of my delusions. Rather than the San Francisco peninsula where they had both been raised, Fran and her husband were living in Nashville, Tennessee where her Rhodes Scholar husband was working as a janitor in one of the recording studios because he had the deranged idea that he wanted to be a musician/singer/songwriter and Nashville was the center of action in that world. Franny was not enamored of life or the culture of Nashville or the sacrifices required for her summa cum laude Rhodes Scholar high school sweetheart husband to pursue the dream of a folk music career. She vented her displeasure of her man, his broom pushing career and the town they lived in. I remember being surprised--she was among the last women I would have imagined in any way to be associated with the counter-culture--but I instinctively felt understanding and kinship with her man and his path. I remember thinking that a Rhodes Scholar who felt strongly enough about his musical talent and ambition to push a broom around a Nashville recording studio in order to study the trade was doing something more than whistling "Dixie" to piss off his wife and that Franny was selling him short. A few years later I heard Franny and her husband were divorced and I was not surprised. It was a few years after that before I became aware that Franny's ex-husband was Kris Kristofferson.

Many years later I saw Kris in concert in Aspen with Judy Collins and I wanted to have the opportunity to tell him this story, but it never happened and I never did.)

My journal entries from that summer include a few observations about people and Chile and my own unfolding awareness of the world and the place I needed to find within it. Technical notes include: "Don't sit too far forward on your skis. This comes from using too much power skiing technique. It's good to get out of trouble on in a difficult, high speed, tight turn. But is slow in races."

And:

"Sit flat on your skis and even slightly back if you can possibly manage it. Your skis are planing in this position and are faster. Your stability is not as steady. But you are light on your skis and in turn able to be quicker....this is very difficult to do correctly. Only a handful of skiers (Stein, Pravda, Sailer, etc.) can do this right. The trick is to maintain control over your skis and at the same time ride far enough back on them to let them get the best possible planing position.

"This becomes increasingly difficult to do as one progresses with it. As one increases his speed he needs more control and better reflexes which are more difficult to co-ordinate in this position. But it is something that must be eventually arrived at."

And:

"FLUSH. "Stein runs a flush unlike most, even the champions of today. But his method is the fastest, I believe, and must, therefore, be assimilated and learned to perfection. It is something that must be learned perfectly or not at all. One mistake denotes a fall. It is quite different. This method relies on quickness and rhythm. Both are important. I don't know how long it will take me to learn this but after two days of practice I feel it will be a long time.

"The method does not use the standard turning through a gate. A flush is not to be run with any turns. You do not enter the 1st gate of the flush low. Instead you enter high like the entering of a correctly run hairpin.

"The correct way depends on a rhythmic stepping through each gate without turning. To do this it must be remembered that while in the flush and coming out of the flush one must carry full speed and will be going 'balls out.' Therefore, according to what speed can be handled through the flush, the speed must be checked down before entering,"

And:

"Stein says that I am too close to the slalom poles. He means that by being 2 inches further away I will be much safer and steadier. For the minute added speed I gain by being that close to the poles I lose more in being unsteady and unsure. But I think I'll stay close to the gate as when I work more at it I'll be able to handle it with only a small amount of risk."

And the best note of the summer, a dim insight into the working of things, an instinctive guide through the difficulties of life, both on and off skis:

"In any combination that is quick it is necessary to begin the movement for the gate in the gate above it. To do this it is sometimes necessary to quit all technique and simply throw oneself into the turn. In such a case the mind is not quick enough to think out the combination and the reflexes and ability of the skier must work for him. To do this you must be relaxed enough and confident enough to let your body take over your mind."

We gringos lived a life of privilege, sleeping and eating and socializing in an elite, elegant hotel by a lovely lake in one of the most beautiful mountain settings I've ever seen. We worked hard at improving our skiing, but not nearly as hard or long as the brown-skinned men and women and boys and girls who prepared and served on white linen tablecloths in a fine dining room our food and drink, made our beds, swept and polished the floors, ran the ski lifts, washed the dishes, cleaned the toilets and changed the towels for less money a day than the cost of one of our meals. It is an old story, the story of mankind, endlessly repeated with no sign of a plot change. The people who made our Portillo existence possible would never know the indulgence of learning the luxury of devoting the major energies of life to something so esoteric and peripheral to the essential as learning the fastest methods of sliding down a snow covered mountain on a pair of turned up sticks. A gringo skier who performed badly or even fell down could and in most cases would go back up and try again. A broken ski could be replaced and every Gringo in Portillo could afford to do so, though for some it would be easier than for others. A broken leg temporarily ended the luxury of skiing while undoubtedly improving the GPA of every skiing college student to have one. A Chilean worker who performed badly or who literally or figuratively fell down on the job would immediately be fired and face hardships unimaginable to and completely unseen by the Norte Americanos esquiadores de Portillo. A broken leg to an uninsured, uneducated Chilean waiter was disaster and perhaps lifelong physical handicap, and the concept of a university education was as unimaginable and unseen to that waiter as the reality of his life was to the Gringoes.

In the case of Portillo the old story went something like this: The first recorded humans around Portillo were the Picunches who arrived around the seventh century A.D. from Peru and were later referred to as Quillatones by the later arriving Spanish. The Picunches appear to have lived peacefully in Aconcagua Valley until the middle of the 15th century when they were overrun by the Inca civilization to the north, from whence, as the old story goes, the Picunches originally came. A century later the Spanish conquered, enslaved, destroyed and plundered the Incas, along with many other cultures and peoples and places throughout South America and Mexico. In due time, the Spanish were tossed out and/or overrun by the citizens of Chile, most of them European immigrants or their descendants, the most notable having the decidedly un-Spanish name of Bernardo O'Higgins. The old story continues: conquerors go to where there is room to expand, wealth to plunder and conquered peoples to do the dirty work of empire. Sometimes the conquered turn the tables and become the conquerors, another turn in an old story.

That first trip to Chile was a great and nurturing experience. The best gift from that time was the awareness of the difference between the never ending path of knowledge within the always growing palace of awareness and the walls of certainty that stop growth and turn the palace into a prison.

I returned from Chile to Reno, resumed my studies at the University of Nevada and threw myself into training for ski racing like never before. I was determined to be ready for the upcoming Olympic tryouts and I was convinced I was capable of making the team. Unfortunately (or not) before the first tryout race I had managed to sabotage my chances of success without having a clue that I had done so with both tactical and strategic errors of judgment, 'errors' being a kind and gentle word to describe a combination of stupidity, immaturity, inattention and the gullibility that accompanies each of them. I might have benefited from some coaching/guidance in matters of ski racing and the larger matters of how to live. That I did not have them was in part but not entirely my own doing. (All of my journals from leaving Chile until the fall of 1961 were stolen by a deranged old woman--more on that in due time--so the writing about this time of life after 50 years and is dependent on the sometimes self-serving imperfections of memory.) The basic tactical ski racing error was to buy new skis for the tryouts, abandoning the ones that had served me well and were far from worn out. In those days of laminated hickory construction every new ski was stiff and would soften (break down) with use. I didn't know and if anyone else knew they kept it to themselves that a softer ski works better, and more to the point of racing was faster than a stiff ski in all but rock hard snow conditions. In the first races of the season I was notably slower than I should have been and I couldn't determine why. Later in the season some of my results improved, but by then I was disappointed, discouraged and puzzled by my poor performances. It would be some ten years later, after I had taught skiing and coached ski racers that I became aware of this elemental aspect of how different skis move over and through snow. Three years later, as noted in my first journal after the old ones were stolen, I was still stewing and trying to understand (and, one could say, rationalize) what had happened to me. This from my new journal of October 27, 1961 while living essentially on the streets of Berkeley/Oakland trying to recover from the personal trauma of divorce, the emotional disappointment and hard, new awareness of friends who were no longer friends in the fallout of the divorce, and the physical trauma of a broken leg that took two years to heal: "I made my bid for skiing in 1959. It was the bid for skiing corresponding to my bid in writing and a way in life now. I tried and had the ability. I just didn't do it. I had spent all that time to be told I wasn't good enough. It was Charlotte's fault for compromising my skiing at that time. It was the weather's fault for such a late winter. It was my fault for losing my past good control on my mind and mental system. Of course there is always the hard fact that I just didn't get down the courses fast enough. But there were reasons because I knew how to get down those courses on time, but just didn't or couldn't....At any rate, that is in the past and I must learn from it. From it I learned that my writing must take precedent over everything and everybody, including myself, in order for it to mean what it must. I learned a lot of other things too. But the placing of values is the most important one."

The strategic error was a girl who would be a woman as I was a boy who would be a man. Her name was Charlotte. When I returned from Chile in the fall of 1958 I began dating Charlotte. I have no memory of how or why that began or what we did on our first date(s), and my journals of that time are gone. I do remember going to the Monterey Jazz Festival and listening to Shelly Manne, Billie Holliday, Cal Tjader, Dave Brubeck, the Modern Jazz Quartet and others with her. It was a great experience for me and I loved the music and enjoyed the girl and we partied and laughed and had a good time. That first Monterey Jazz Festival was the first weekend in October and by the end of November Charlotte and I were clandestinely fucking in the back seat of our cars and, on occasion, renting a motel room and spending the night, and, as was customary in that time, pretending it wasn't happening. We had known each other since the beginning of high school, and she had lived less than a block away that first year in Reno, but we had never had any relationship deeper than a friendly acquaintanceship until that fall. Charlotte, an honors student, was voted the outstanding girl in our Reno High School graduating class of 1956 and had moved on to Stanford University where she lived when we started dating. She was a brilliant student, a good person, a fun-loving girl. Had she not gotten involved with me, she likely would have gone on to earn a PhD and live a very different life than the one she did. But that fall we became enamored of each other and that magnetism skewed the compasses of both our paths, diluting the focus and intensity of both her studies and my ski racing. She favored skiing and loved to party and did not seem to mind if I drove fast. We had fun together. She grasped the importance of ski racing and writing to my life. I admired her academic abilities. She understood and accepted the inherent consequences and cost of being with an angry young man at odds with his society who wished to ski race and write instead of carving a bourgeois career out of an obdurate cultural fabric with the graceless tools of social ambition. Or so it seemed at the time. I was 20 when we got married in 1959, 21 when our son, Scott, was born, and 22 when we divorced.

Only one of my older friends attempted to deter me from getting too involved with Charlotte. That was Rusty Crook, five years my senior, a good friend and an older mentor in skiing and life. Rusty saw that despite Charlotte's intelligence, integrity and charm, she was socially respectable, ambitious and conforming in ways that I would never be. Charlotte and I were and are as different as oil and water. Some 40 years later the son Charlotte and I had, Scott, observed to me, "I don't see how you two could ever be in the same room together, much less have a conversation." He said it without rancor and with respect and affection for us both.

Nevertheless, in the middle of the Olympic tryouts, on the way to Sun Valley for the Harriman Cup, one of the best and most important of the season's tryout races, we took a clandestine detour to Jerome, Idaho and were secretly married in the courthouse by the Justice of the Peace. (Though I wouldn't learn of it for a couple of years and not meet him for nearly 40 years, my second son was born the day before my first marriage.) After the Harriman Cup, at which I skied poorly, Charlotte returned to Stanford and I continued on the circuit to Colorado and New England. It was a frustrating and disappointing season of racing for me and it left me more adrift, unfocused and dissatisfied than I had been in my entire life, not the state of mind or spirit of life one would expect of a newlywed. I was 20 years old.

Chapter IV
THE FIRST MARRIAGE

Didn't turn out so well.

When I returned to the west in a 65 hour drive from upstate New York to Reno after the racing season was over I was naturally excited to see my secret new bride and continue with our relationship and unfolding lives. At the age of 20 I had preconceptions and expectations of a hidden marriage between two people who were destined to live very different lives in different places that were unrealistic, immature, riven with organic fault lines and not shared by my secret bride. Suffice it to say that within a few weeks it was clear to me that our marriage was a grave mistake and that I was not ready to be married to anyone. I don't pretend to speak for Charlotte but, in my opinion, neither was she. I proposed we go about having the marriage annulled and get on with our respective lives. That would have been the correct, honorable, practical correction to an immature blunder, but if we had done that our son Scott would not have been born and Scott, in addition to being a son we love, is a fine, dynamic and productive presence in our lives and the larger world. Life has its own reasons, costs and rewards.

I wanted to annul the marriage (without having a clue about how to do that), not mention it to our families or friends and get on with our respective lives as if it hadn't happened. But Charlotte had a different relationship with her parents than I did with mine and she was not willing to put the marriage behind us as a youthful mistake. She went to her parents and told them what we had done. Faster than I had ever left a ski race starting gate I was involved in a flurry of meetings with Charlotte and her mother (who never liked me and the feeling was reciprocal), Charlotte and her father (who did like me and the feeling was reciprocal) and Charlotte and the minister of the Methodist church where Charlotte's mother was the organist. The talks with the minister could not include the information that we were already married. The gist of the ones with her parents was that since Charlotte and I had slept together and were married we should not annul the marriage but, instead, have another marriage, a large, public, phony one in the Methodist Church. It was the sex that troubled her parents and made an annulment so distasteful to them. We never told them we had been sleeping together before the marriage or that neither of us were virgins before that. It was simply assumed. That I already had sired two sons by the time this slapstick tragedy was unfolding is an irony that, had any of us known about them, would have changed everyone's perspective and enthusiasm for the public marriage. It is one of the times in life when I did not hold my ground when I should have and I knew it was a mistake, but....................I did not.

That summer we had a huge wedding at the Reno Methodist Church presided over by the Methodist minister, followed by a reception in Charlotte's parents' back yard and a weekend honeymoon on the west shore of Lake Tahoe. We rented an apartment in Reno and I worked as the head of advertising at a newspaper in Fallon, 60 miles to the east. I commuted five days a week. Charlotte had a job but I cannot remember what it was. We worked and came home and lived like I imagine most newly wedded couples with jobs do. On weekends we partied with friends and took some hikes in the nearby Sierra Nevada where I was most comfortable. I have two strong memories of that time in the apartment: the first was one evening when Charlotte was cooking dinner and suddenly through some mishap of grease or gas her hair was on fire and she screamed and I grabbed her head and put it under the water spigot in the sink which quickly and without damage to her extinguished the fire in her hair; the second, probably a month after our second, phony wedding, I woke up early one morning and watched her for several minutes sleeping beside me. She was a decent and unusually intelligent young woman of mainstream, traditional values and goals I did not share, and I knew without doubt that we could not be together and that I was not where or with whom I belonged and that we had made (another) great mistake and should have pursued my annulment idea of the spring. I woke her and explained (again) my feelings and thoughts, which, in addition to my values and goals, she did not share. From the perspective of more than 50 years after the fact, it is clear to me that we both did our best in the situation to do the 'right' thing. But she was only 21 and I 20 and we had very different concepts of 'right' and 'wrong.' It was a long summer. By the end of it I knew that I was not an advertising man, that I was not Charlotte's man and that I had made a muddle of my life before I had even become a man.

Rather than clean up the mess before it got messier we continued with the disorder. We decided that Charlotte would return to Stanford and her studies, I would stay in Reno and continue my studies at the University of Nevada, and we would pretend we were still together in hearts and minds. She left and I stayed, but not for long. A month into the semester I simply couldn't continue to live in a manner and place where my heart wasn't. I phoned my old friend, Stein Eriksen, the greatest ski racer of his time, and asked him for a job. Stein ran the ski school and ski shop at Aspen Highlands in Aspen and he offered me the job of running the rental/repair shop for the winter. I could go to work as soon as I could get to Aspen. I quit school, packed up and got ready to leave, but before that I somehow had it in my head that the 'right' thing to do was go to Palo Alto for a meeting with Charlotte to clarify what I was doing. We spent a few days together and agreed that we would not be together and agreed to deal with the messy details of divorce/annulment/social turmoil at an indeterminate future time. We weren't together and would not be together but since we were together for a few days we slept together as if we were together. Obviously, we didn't have our acts, minds or hearts together. I left Palo Alto and went to Aspen in late October 1959. Aspen was wonderful and I felt better about life and myself than I had in nearly a year. I rented an inexpensive room in the private home where three years earlier Ron Funk, Tony Perry and I had spent the winter. My landlords were wonderful and glad to see me, and I spent the pre-snow weeks setting up the shop in Highlands, taking long hikes in the hills, reading and both reveling and relaxing in the culture and landscape of the world in which I was most comfortable.

After the rigors of the previous several months, of the damages to psyche, perspective and self-confidence and of giving in where I knew I should not, spending solitary time with and both nurturing and healing my better self was refreshing, revealing and very, very healthy. I was consciously happy for the first time in too long.

Eventually it snowed, Highlands opened and we arranged that everyone who worked in the shop had a few hours each day to ski. I worked and skied and read and wrote and kept my social engagements to a minimum, taking the time to reevaluate the things of life and possible directions to take them. It was a wonderful time.

It didn't last very long.

Just before Christmas Charlotte informed me that she had gotten pregnant during our last visit in Palo Alto and she wanted to come to Aspen to talk about it. I agreed and during her Christmas break from Stanford she came to Aspen. Understandably, it was an emotionally tumultuous meeting, some of it nutritious, much of it confusing and all of it laced with the implacable if unacknowledged larger dynamics of our relationship. We spent a week discussing and doing our best to come to grips with an increasingly complex situation. We were both 21 years old and I think had good intentions and did our individual best to do 'the right thing.' In many ways our friendship, which was not the same things as our married/romantic relationship, was on the most solid footing it had ever been or ever would be. I don't remember the specifics of our conversations or how we came to the conclusions we did, but we agreed that for the sake of our unborn child we should do our best to make our marriage work. So........we agreed that I would stay in Aspen, Charlotte would return to Palo Alto, quit school (one semester from graduating as an honor student), move to Aspen where we would establish a household as expectant parents and live happily ever after in the mountain/ski world that was my home, inspiration, culture and, in so many ways, family. She left with the understanding and, I believe, intention of returning in a couple of weeks with her belongings and I readied myself for a different life.

And it didn't last very long.

Again, I don't remember specific details, but sometime after the agreed upon time had passed with no sign of Charlotte we spoke by phone. She informed me that she stopped in Reno to visit and discuss the situation with her parents and they decided the better course of action was for Charlotte to return to Stanford, finish her studies and I should move to Palo Alto to be with her. It would be some 20 years before I understood and appreciated the significance 'they' in the previous sentence exerted on the dynamics of what I thought of as a private, personal, one-on-one relationship with my wife. My relationship with my own parents had allowed me to reach the age of 21 largely naïve about the dynamics of more traditional, mainstream families of America. I would no more have turned to my parents for advice on marriage or relationships than I had relied on Les Hawkins for information about skiing. Their knowledge as expressed by example was not of interest to me, and, for better and worse, richer and poorer, I had learned early in life to have a healthy distrust of authority. But Charlotte's model of marriage was that of her parents, Clarence and Martha, whose love and approval she sought with all the power of her intellectual gifts and the desire of the youngest, least favorite daughter. That it would be folly for Charlotte to curtail her education at Stanford was, of course, good advice. Her considerable intellectual potential would be wasted, unexplored and left fallow in Aspen, as would my soul in Palo Alto. The thought of living in Palo Alto was repugnant to me and, as we had already proven, living together was not fulfilling to either of us. I told her that if she wanted to move to Aspen I would do my best to make a life with her, but I could no more leave my mountains than she could leave her education. Nor, in retrospect, should either of us have done so. She was going to stay in Palo Alto. I was going to stay in Aspen and I wanted a divorce.

Impasse.

There was more to the distance between us than the miles between California and Colorado and so it would have remained if I had not, just a month later, badly broken my leg and ankle in a ski race in Alta, Utah. It was the National Championship downhill and I was pushing harder than my recent training regimen gave me the freedom to push. The break required surgery, screws, a plate and I spent several days recovering in a Salt Lake City hospital before being allowed to leave. My surgeon, a skier who had watched the fall, informed me after surgery that I would likely not be able to ski for five years and would never ski race again. I knew he was wrong even as he said it, but his outlook did not improve my spirits or options. I don't remember how it played out, but Charlotte drove to Salt Lake and picked me up and we drove back to Palo Alto to set up a new life as expectant parents away from the mountains that were my home, in upward mobility upper middle-class suburbia where I did not belong or wish to be.

Ken Kesey lived just a few miles away at the time, but like most of the world I did not know him or of him or what he was up to, and it would be several years before I began to catch up with Kesey and his perspective and, metaphorically, get on the bus. Still, there were several very good things about the time in Palo Alto. The best was the approaching arrival of our child, Charlotte's first. I thought at the time it was my first but later learned that Scott Howard Dorworth (later Markewitz) born on July 3, 1960 at Stanford Hospital was my third son.

I got a job with the Sociology Department at Stanford University while Charlotte finished her studies and I coped with a white plaster cast and an equally stifling alien culture and landscape. It was a fascinating job, almost worth the injury and having to live in Palo Alto. The head of Stanford's Sociology Department at that time was a brilliant man by the name of Sanford Dornbusch. He made a lasting impression on me, and, I'm positive, many of his students. In one class I watched the good professor drive home a point about the relationship between charismatic leaders and the masses which follow, and, therefore, the nature of man. He stood behind a wooden podium in front of a class of about 30 and delivered a dry, scholarly lecture on the phenomenon of evangelicals. What he was really up to was neither dry nor intellectual. It was visceral and frightening and I had never seen anything like it before. Or, rather, I had seen it before and see it still, but Dornbusch made me aware of what I was truly seeing. I am grateful for that awareness. He started out with an unadorned historical account of the evangelical movement in America. Then he moved on to the message delivered by evangelists and the group hysteria and personal and group metamorphosis it can create in the audience. He implied without saying so that the evangelical congregation is usually composed of the uneducated, the superstitious and the unsophisticated. His students accepted without question, a pause or a close look the implication that this could not describe a class of Stanford students. Dornbusch was a powerful speaker and his class was riveted by his words as he moved to the techniques used by evangelists, claiming the power of the omniscient, rhythm, tone of voice, provoking the human desire for what believers call 'salvation' and others term a 'clear conscience.'

But Dornbusch was up to something very different than narrative history. He was a sociology professor, his subject the behavior of living people, not an account of dead ones. Dornbusch was a kind of genius of his trade. With a quiet subtlety used more often by musicians than university lecturers, he had been softly, slowly tapping a beat with one finger from the beginning of his oration. As the talk progressed he switched to two fingers, pounded so delicately beneath the power of his voice, that no one was conscious of the beat. By the time he spoke of rhythm and tone of voice, he had been lightly and rhythmically rapping the podium for fifteen minutes. When he switched to slapping his hand on the wood to keep the beat, raising his voice in time with the cadence, his audience was already mesmerized. He had them, literally, in the palm of his hand. It was the work of a performing magician, contrived and manipulated (and manipulative). The entire class was soon clapping in time with the rhythm and answering in the affirmative that they believed. For that moment, they did. In half an hour a class of Stanford students was transformed from the country's economic/intellectual elite into yeaaaaing, witnessing, stomping members of a revival meeting worthy of the most soundly thumped bible in the most tattered tent set up in the most barren field of America's uneducated, unsophisticated, primal heartland. Sociology 101.

It was a masterful show.

And then he stopped.

Silence enveloped the room. Professor and students regarded each other with new attentiveness and the ancient wariness that always accompanies fresh knowledge of things not being as they appear. The thin veneer of civilization---that layer of education, social protocol, laws, organized religion, class and family hierarchy, tradition, ritual, myths, art and the like---was seen to be permeable and fragile, almost a dream. The social deceit of a safe, manageable, predictable world, where pain is avoided and pleasure and security gained by effort and intelligent, socially responsible action, was revealed as self-serving hypocrisy, a smug lie. Even the small, privileged group of people whose material/intellectual good fortune would land them in a sociology class at Stanford University is separated by the flimsiest of illusions from crass superstition, mass hysteria and profound self-deception. In fact, they are not separated at all.

Indeed, when the illusion vanishes, in significant ways the inner world of human civilization has evolved less than it supposes, and America's Puritan based society is still rooted in the same forces and horrors that created the Salem Witch Trials. The security all societies seek and some maintain is held together as much by pretense, denial and repression as by law and order, compassion and justice.

Next to the presence of our son, I am most grateful to the Stanford co-ed for the opportunity to learn something of this. It would prove helpful in both surviving and understanding the events and evolution of my own life and the currents and content of my society. While she embraced and embodied the contradictions and hypocrisies of that society while I rejected and fought with them, neither of us are or were or ever will be separate from that culture. There is always an individual, experiential price to be paid for however one chooses to relate to the larger society. For reasons I am still discovering, I could not pay in the coin of conformity, and not many months after Dornbush's classroom revival meeting I left the co-ed and our infant son. At first it was an amiable if distressing split, and she drove me to Lake Tahoe and the mountains that I missed and needed and would never really leave again, mountains that meant as little to her as her social respectability did to me. She pulled the car over in Tahoe Valley, and I got out along the road with a suitcase of clothes, a typewriter, less than $100 and no plan. After a tearful farewell she drove away with Scott in the back seat in a bassinet. It was the first son I knew I was leaving behind, though exactly who was leaving who behind is an open question. The end of a marriage shares obvious metaphors with dropping an atomic bomb but what was never in question in my mind is that, despite the difficulties and pain, splitting the nuclear family was in the best interests of father, son, mother and the larger society.

I never looked back.

BOOK Five

Chapter I
YIN

"Often, moreover, it is...that aspect of our being that society finds eccentric, ridiculous, or disagreeable, that holds our sweet waters, our secret well of happiness, the key to our equanimity in malevolent climes."
Tom Robbins

"Someone I loved once gave me a box full of darkness. It took me years to understand that this too, was a gift."
Mary Oliver

"What hurts you, blesses you. Darkness is your candle."
Rumi

It was, obviously, a defining moment. Another occurred less than five minutes later, a serendipitous event that would alter my life in unimaginable ways. I was still standing by the side of Highway 50 pondering my next move and reveling in the breathing of fresh mountain air and looking at pine trees and mountains when Ron Funk walked out of the woods. He was just finishing a hike. I thought I might be hallucinating. "Hey, man, what are you doing?" he queried. I didn't really know, but within ten minutes of Charlotte leaving me by the side of the road and driving away I had a friend, a place to live, the mountains and, a few days later, a job. It was late summer, 1960.

We had not been in communication for more than a year and I had no idea where Ron was or what doing, but he was working at South Shore for a mutual friend's construction company and was happy to see me. He had a small house with a spare room and invited me to stay in it. Within a couple of days the mutual friend offered me a job as well. In the space of a few days I went from living in an unhealthy, dysfunctional, dark personal situation in a city as uncomfortable for me as the situation itself to the mountains which I loved, living with a kindred spirit friend who understood through his own experience my mental, emotional, spiritual and, as an oft-injured ski racer, physical predicament. Ron's friendship was a bright ray of sunshine in a dark time of life and helped me heal and find my way. Mom and Dad and the majority of my old, trusted friends were disappointed, unhappy and angry with me for leaving Charlotte and for the person I was becoming, and my old circle of Reno friends was more disapproving than welcoming or comforting. A few weeks later I re-injured my leg at work and was no longer able to work, and decided to return to college in Reno to finish my University education. I moved into a small apartment with three of those friends without understanding the dynamics of our relationships had unalterably changed. Since one of them was dating and later married one of Charlotte's best friends who was and is among my longest standing and strongest critics, it was not a good living situation for me or them. I don't think any of us grasped those changes at first, but in due time I felt like a Pariah in my own social circle and, naturally, moved on.

This Haiku from Buson (1716-1783) comes to mind:

Through snow,
Lights of homes
That slammed their gates on me.

I went to school, studied, partied, worked a few odd jobs, dated, worked out as best my damaged leg would allow, and labored to reconstruct a life from the debris with all the skills and imagination of a pissed off 21 year old.

One night during this unsettled time I ran into Farol on the streets of Reno while prowling the bars in search of answers and relief that were not there. She invited me to have a beer. We retired to one of Reno's quiet bars and she told me she had gotten pregnant that spring we had dated. She knew I was neither interested in nor amenable to fatherhood, husbandhood or domesticity, so she managed to have the child (a boy) and put him up for adoption at birth without letting her family or friends (except for one, an old boy friend, who helped her with logistics) know about it, a neat trick in 1950s Nevada. She told me the date and town of our son's birth, and she wanted me to know that she was very proud of our son and had no regrets, much as she would miss his presence in her life. I remembered the date and city of our son's birth and wondered how he was doing and where and what he looked like and what sort of person he was becoming. It didn't occur to me that I would or could ever know, though more than 30 years later I did.

During this time Charlotte was in Palo Alto and we spoke by phone once a week and I was able to see Scott when she visited her parents in Reno and a few times when I went to Palo Alto. We had long discussions about the details of the divorce we needed to have and, as such things go, they seemed to me to be caring, intelligent and civil if not entirely agreeable talks. Among other things we agreed that I would make child support payments but would not pay alimony. The reasoning behind this covenant was that she had a fine education from one of the best universities in America, a job, economic ambition and was a daughter of wealth. I had at least two years remaining at a less prestigious university as an English major before graduation (it took three years, as it worked out) and was not connected to financial stability by either ambition or genetics and had never pretended otherwise. We agreed and even laughed about the absurdity of me paying alimony. At the time of our talks I had every intention of staying connected to Scott in all ways, including financial, and I believed Charlotte shared that intention.

One afternoon that autumn at the small apartment in Reno my studying was interrupted by a knock at the door. It was a summons server with divorce papers Charlotte had filed in California. He was extremely courteous and apologized for having to serve such papers on anyone. It was his profession and he had served such papers many times and I appreciated his demeanor, signed for the receipt of the divorce summons, thanked him for his consideration and took the papers inside and read them.

They changed our lives in ways that neither Charlotte nor I, nor the legal/societal process of divorce, intended. The divorce papers asked for a reasonable amount of money each month for child support as well as a small amount each month for alimony. I thought there must have been a mistake and phoned Charlotte. She informed me there was no mistake and that she had included alimony on the advice of her lawyer to ignore the agreement she and I had made. I have forgotten how many times we went back and forth on this issue but I eventually spoke by phone with her lawyer who informed me I would pay the alimony and agree to the divorce terms or I would wind up in jail. He also explained that increasing the amount of alimony payments as time went on was easier than increasing child support payments, thus his advice to his client. With all the maturity of an angry, immature 21 year old, the frustration of having another much discussed agreement with Charlotte broken on the advice of someone else, the same instinctive wisdom that caused me to flee the Christian Brothers and the unreserved glee of speaking richly obscene laced truth to disrespectful and thereby disrespected power, I informed Charlotte's lawyer that he would see me in Mexico before he would see me in jail and hung up. I then repeated the message with fewer obscenities to the lawyer's client and told her if she wanted to abide by the agreement she and I had made between us I would do my best to cooperate and be part of Scott's life. If not, she and her advisor were going to have neither my money (such as it was) nor cooperation (ditto). Soon the divorce was granted on their terms without my acknowledgement or assistance. To her credit (and my benefit) Charlotte never tried to have me jailed, but it would be almost 20 years before we had another decent conversation or honest attempt at communication.

It was a dark time.

Living with three old friends who were no longer friends was a stressful, moderately uncomfortable, practical solution to four young men trying to finish college and find their way in life. There was enough relationship remaining that they did not kick me out and get another roommate, as I think and felt at the time they wanted, and I remember both gratitude and resentment for their practical kindness. The experience added a layer of thickness to my thin skin and was reminder of both the necessity and costs of staying on the path of being true to oneself. Though the costs were proving (and proved) to be more than anticipated, even then I did not blame Charlotte, my parents, friends and judgmental acquaintances for their scorn, disapproval and rejection, at least not entirely. I myself did not want or approve of being separated from my son, but if there was another path I could not see it—then or now.

The best part of those few months were a few new friends in the art department, primarily Joan Arrizabalaga, Ed Martinez and Ron Moroni, whose energies revolved around art, literature and the process of viewing the world as cornucopia rather than commodity and whose company I cherished. We spent a lot of time together, much of it partying, discussing our lives and what to do with them, exploring personal inner landscapes more than the cultural infrastructure, and laughing, always laughing. I worked out on a leg far from healed, not reliable or close to ski racing shape, but the first snows allowed me to make a few turns and I knew in my intact and broken bones and healing soul that skiing and I had many miles yet to go. Another new friend, Dave Sharpe, was a huge help to me in the healing process. Dave was the best miler on the University track team and somehow--even when healthy I am a slow and inept runner--we became running friends and he introduced me to one of the hardest, healthiest, most healing activities a damaged leg (and everything attached to it) could endure: uphill wind sprints in sand. There are some sand dunes on the Mt. Rose Highway between Reno and Lake Tahoe. I had skied on them often early in the season when only a few inches of snow covered the mountains and the sand beneath protected both ski and skier from rocky damage. It never occurred to me to hike up them without snow on top, much less *run* up them, over and over and over and over, but Dave Sharpe convinced me that sand dune uphill wind sprints were for me. He got the idea from the training methods of Herb Elliott of Australia, the greatest middle distance runner of his time, who was introduced to sand hill running by his coach Percy Cerutty. It was a great workout on a damaged leg without undue impact, and I've always been grateful to Dave for his friendship, encouragement and knowledge and to Percy and Herb for passing it on. Improvement in the condition of the physical never leaves out the heart, and mine, as always in the mountains, combined with unease in Reno and disapproval from people there who mattered, directed me to follow its unerring beat and wisdom. At the end of that semester I quit school once again and moved back to Aspen.

I arrived in Aspen via train and bus with a few clothes, a pair of skis, not much money, no plan and the deepest happiness I'd known since leaving a year before. Life in Aspen fell into place with a synchronicity akin to Ron Funk walking out of the woods by Highway 50 and providing the answers to his own question: "Hey, Man, What are you doing?" Within a few days I'd found a place to live in a small house with two old ski racing friends, Don McKinnon and Don Brooks. Through McKinnon who was already working there I landed a job as a beer waiter in the Red Onion, the center of Aspen après ski and night life and folk/rock/jazz entertainment. We worked from 3:30 to 8 p.m., earned enough money to get by and because of tips even save some, were given a free dinner after work and listened to soulful music of that time and beautiful place. Our bartenders were Bill Marolt, whose sons Max and Bill Jr. were among the best and most influential American skiers of their times, and Koji Kataoka.

The greatest American ski racer of the 1930s, Dick Durrance, was by then a fine filmmaker who needed a skier for an Aspen promotional film and I got the job. It included some money for days worked and ski lift pass for the season. The film plot was simple: It involved me and a girl on skis. I was talking with a lovely young woman at the top of Aspen Mountain after getting off the lift. We were laughing and flirting and acting like young skiers do on a sunny day with excellent snow at the top of one of America's best skiing mountains. Suddenly, she rips the hat off my head and takes off skiing down the mountain, laughing and holding the hat aloft. I give chase. I spent the entire winter on those days when the weather was perfect chasing Sherry Gerbaz down Aspen

Mountain on skis in pursuit of my hat for Dick Durrance's camera. It was great fun and Dick and his wife Miggs became life long friends. We usually skied in powder snow which was easy for my damaged leg. I entered a few ski races with discouraging results, but I was doing far better than the surgeon who had operated on the leg had predicted and I took heart in that. 'Take heart' is not an empty admonition. I never did see the film Dick made from that footage but the making of it was fine physical therapy, and, as I was coming to learn and am still learning, the physical is inextricably connected to the mental, emotional, spiritual, social and cultural.

The happiness, well-being, sense of community and belonging, vitality and wholeness experienced that winter in Aspen was a stark, noted contrast to the quality of my life in Reno and Palo Alto. At 22 I was beginning to experience as an individual some of the seismic shifts that in the next decade would divide our country along love/hate war/peace freedom/authoritarianism material/spiritual environmental/ profit cultural/counter-cultural fault lines. The same month I moved to Aspen John Kennedy was sworn in as U.S. President and out-going President Eisenhower famously told congress, "In the councils of government, we must guard against the acquisition of unwarranted influence, whether sought or unsought, by the militaryindustrial complex. The potential for the disastrous rise of misplaced power exists and will persist." (As we experienced in Viet Nam, Iraq, Afghanistan and elsewhere 'we' did not stand sufficient guard against the militaryindustrial complex and its civilian arm the NRA, and the country and the world has paid and continues to pay dearly for such callous carelessness, some more than others.) The Bay of Pigs invasion of Cuba occurred that year. The Freedom Riders began bus rides of integration into the south and the Civil Rights Movement in America began. Bob Dylan moved to New York City but we didn't know about him for a couple of years. Timothy Leary, Richard Alpert and others had started a research project called the Harvard Psilocybin Project, but we didn't learn about that for a couple of years either. But we were already tuning into the personal dynamics of what became some of Leary's best known (and, if taken to heart and mind, nutritional) quotes:

"Think for yourself and question authority."

"Women who seek to be equal with men lack ambition."

"You're only as young as the last time you changed your mind."

Sometime that winter a parcel of land in downtown Aspen was for sale. I don't remember the details of who was selling it or why, but I remember the price of $6000 and exactly where it is. Since I was happy and loved Aspen I decided that I would try to buy the land and start making a life in Aspen as entrepreneur---or something. I asked my aunt Llewellyn to loan me the money and told her why, and in earlier years I am confident she would have done so. But my beloved aunt was as disappointed, dismayed and disapproving of me as so many others and she turned me down, though she went out of her way to make it clear that while she didn't understand or approve of what I was doing with myself she still loved me. I was mildly disappointed and more than gently encouraged by her expressions of love, and, most important to me, kindly informed that disapproval did not necessarily carry rejection, lack of respect or isolation. (That property is now worth around 10 million dollars and it is clear to me that my lovely aunt did me a great favor by not allowing me to get caught in a path of life measured in dollars.) When the ski season ended I stayed around Aspen for several weeks, working on the home Dick and Miggs were building on Red Mountain, before moving on. I don't remember why I returned west but the ski season was over and I was adrift and the tides were probably driven by Uncle Harvey's expansion of his casino at South Shore where Llewellyn made sure I got a well-paying construction job working on the project.

Brooks and McKinnon joined me and found jobs and the three of us rented a small house at South Shore within a few blocks of where I had lived and attended grammar school after WWII, where a year earlier Charlotte had dropped me off on the highway, Ron Funk had walked out of the woods, and, many years before, Doug Gaynor had introduced me to the world of skiing. As Thomas Wolfe eloquently pointed out, you can't go home again, but you certainly can wander around the neighborhood again and again. And I did. Each weekday morning Brooks, McKinnon and I rose early and went our separate ways to the work of hard labor for good pay. Though the work was physically demanding, most days when I returned to the cabin I did some form of training exercise—a run, hike, calisthenics—before drinking a six-pack of beer, reading, writing in my journals and then to bed. On weekends we partied, hiked in the Sierra, went to the Tahoe beaches and talked about the events and meanings and choices of our young, unfolding lives. Paul Ryan, an east coast ski racer who was part of our group of friends who trained and socialized together in Aspen, was visiting us when we heard that Ernest Hemingway had committed suicide and we all drank beers in commemoration of a great writer and troubled man. In different ways, we were (are?) all troubled. Brooks, an outlaw at heart who used a simmering anger to justify a larcenous streak, spent one weekend stealing a boat from one of the Tahoe marinas on a Friday night, driving it to his hometown of Portland, selling it and returning to work Monday morning with more cash than he could earn in a month of construction. I disapproved and told him so but wished him luck in not getting caught. He didn't, but several years later went to prison for the crime of being a marijuana smuggler/merchant, a profession that is now legal in several states (as it should be). While in prison Don discovered Jesus. After serving his time he became a good, hard-working, honest citizen, proselytized his religious beliefs to anyone who would listen until you told him to shut up at which point he would smile and return to the good friend and man I'd always known. Don married and then ski raced to the end of his life which happened when his heart stopped during dinner and he dropped face first into his plate in front of his wife with a fork full of food in his hand.

McKinnon spent most of his life in Aspen where he skied, partied, lived the good life, became a successful photographer until Florida's charms and warmth enticed him away from the mountain to the sea. From there my old friend sails and fishes and socializes in the local pubs and sends me fine photos and messages of cheer from both the old and the new days.

It was a good summer in many ways but, like many good things, it didn't last long. I had been getting periodic cortisone shots in my ankle and, while they seemed to help, the combination of working construction all day, working out with the goal of getting strong enough to actually train, and in general trying to live as if my body and psyche were far healthier than they were was rife with risks and never without pain. It ended in August while carrying a heavy beam across the construction yard when I stepped on a board with an unseen nail sticking up. The nail went through the sole of my shoe, through the foot and out the top of the shoe. It hurt like hell and a couple of fellow construction workers pulled the nail and the board out, and that was the end of my job. Fortunately, it was my right and good foot and the primary treatment was tetanus shots. Unfortunately, I was physically unable to do much for awhile.

Not long after this event the draft board requested my presence for a physical. By this time my deepening cynicism about the chasm between the professed and the actual values, practices and true history of my country and society had extended to the U.S. military industry that 'we' had failed to guard against and there was no way I was willingly going to give even a couple years of my life to it. Though I don't remember knowing about it or thinking about its ramifications, more than 2000 U.S. military 'advisors' were already in Viet Nam laying the groundwork for what all too soon became the Viet Nam War, America's disgraceful, unnecessary and defining disaster of the 1960s. Late that summer the Berlin Wall was built. Carl Jung died that year and America's 'Freedom Riders' were being burned, beaten, jailed and killed in the south for their efforts to turn the second paragraph of the United States Declaration of Independence from hypocrisy into reality. Someone (I've always been curious about whom) alerted the draft board that I was no longer married and that the marriage deferment no longer applied to me. I was informed of my new status and dutifully showed up at the draft board in Oakland a few weeks later. It was a surreal experience. Along with dozens of young men from across the spectrum of American society, I stood in long lines and sat in orderly arranged desks being examined and tested to see if we were capable of performing the rudiments of at least training for military service. Two recruits stand out in memory: In one line where we were all dressed only in underwear and holding our clothes I stood next to a man/boy a couple of years younger than me who appeared malnourished, confused, scared and incompetent. I had the thought that if one were about to embark on a combat patrol with this man/boy the safety of the entire patrol would necessitate breaking his leg before starting so that he could not participate. The other memorable recruit sat next to me for one of the written tests and informed me he badly wanted to pass and be in the military but could not understand the questions on the test. I helped him as best I could under the not very watchful eyes of the military personnel in charge with the hope that he might find a place that would protect him. Both of these young gentlemen passed. I did not.

Instead, I was required to report a few days later to the Letterman Army Hospital at the Presidio in San Francisco for a more thorough physical on just my leg. In order to prepare for this encounter with the undesirable military, the day before the physical I rose early and spent the day walking on concrete from North Gate of the University of California Campus in Berkeley to San Leandro and back, a distance of more than 25 miles. Then I went to a favorite Berkeley watering hole and got as drunk as possible, slept a few hours and got myself to Letterman's for the physical with an appalling hangover and an ankle that looked more like a grapefruit than a moveable connection between a human foot and leg. I don't remember the details of having the draft status of both 1Y and 4F, but my (new) journal of October 17, 1961 reports: "Our government gave me a birthday present yesterday. A notice from the draft board declaring me 4-F. Hallelujah you bastard of a govt.! You screw me at every turn; it's about time I had one on you. Since I won't have to fear the draft, I must plan on something to do and a place to go after this semester is over. Perhaps Mexico."

I never heard from the draft board again, though a few years later I came to have good reason to believe that my file was surreptitiously removed without my knowledge from the draft board offices and probably burned.

Chapter II
CRAWLING TOWARD YANG

"It is always darkest just before the Day dawneth."
Thomas Fuller: "A Pisgah-Sight Of Palestine And The
Confines Thereof", 1650

*"This is the secret of the golden flower: if the heart can die the
flower will bloom, die as you are so you can be reborn."*
Osho: "The Secret of Secrets

In retrospect, it is clear that at the point of the nail going through my foot I lost heart, gave up and said 'fuck it' for the next several months. What I didn't see at the time was that among the things I was saying 'fuck it" to was the effort of being true to myself. I had enough money saved from working at Uncle Harvey's to get me through a few months, but it was a grim dark period. For reasons I don't remember and can't imagine now but probably connected with the draft board physicals in the Bay Area, I wound up living in cheap flop houses in Oakland and on friends' couches and beds in Berkeley, eating the least expensive food I could find and drinking lots of beer. I took night classes at the University of California at Berkeley in Spanish, French Literature and Art Appreciation, and the bright lights of a dark time were those classes (especially art appreciation), long walks and, eventually, runs in the hills and streets of Berkeley and the Bancroft Library where I spent afternoons reading the recently published collected letters of Vincent Van Gogh. His art, which at that point I'd only seen in reproductions, was among my favorites and moved, inspired and intrigued me like no other.

His writings had a similar effect except the written word and Van Gogh's life and personality connected with me in different ways than his wonderful paintings. Since childhood times in the snowbound days of Tahoe, the written word was my preferred choice of both expression and acquisition of understanding the myriad ways of the world and its inhabitants. During dark times searching for light Van Gogh was a good companion of mind and spirit.

My old ski racing friend, Paul Ryan, was attending graduate film school at San Francisco State University and I sometimes camped on the couch of his small San Francisco apartment. It was my favorite among the kaleidoscopic living arrangements of those few months, and Paul was and is a gem and a good friend. He went on to have a highly successful career as a filmmaker, motion picture photographer and still photographer both in the world of skiing and the larger arena of Hollywood. An on-line magazine describes Paul's career: "Fueled by the revolutionary changes occurring in film during the late Sixties, Ryan...was subsequently given a rare opportunity to combine his twin passions when he was commissioned to make a documentary about the European ski racing circuit. 'The first plastic ski boots were invented by a company called Lange,' he recalls. 'They were so far ahead in their industry that literally 80 percent of the ski racers in the world wore their boots. They had more money than they knew what to do with. I already knew a lot of the guys in ski racing, so the Lange people said to me, 'Why don't you make us a film about it? Show the boots every now and then, but just go and do it.' So I basically had a blank check to go to Europe and follow the racing circuit for six weeks! Nowadays, no one would give a green kid just out of film school that kind of freedom.'

"Ryan used the opportunity to break away from the previously staid conventions of sports filmmaking and experiment with the gonzo visual ideas that were invigorating the greater film world at the time. He cites the cinema verité styles pioneered by Jean-Luc Godard and the Maysles brothers, replete with jump cuts and other non-traditional film language, as inspirations. The result of Ryan's efforts, Ski Racer, went on to become a classic of the nascent ski documentary genre. Ryan's success led to further documentary work, with subjects ranging from the Hell's Angels in San Francisco to artist Salvador Dali at his home in Spain.

"After landing a job shooting production stills on George Lucas' classic American Graffiti, Ryan's appetite was whetted for feature-film work. He got his opportunity when director Terence Malick asked him to handle second-unit direction and cinematography on the film Days of Heaven (shot by Nestor Almendros, ASC, and Haskell Wexler, ASC), which earned an Academy Award for Best Cinematography."

It can easily be argued that Paul's "Ski Racer" changed the world of ski films and that many of today's best and classic ski films are spiritual and technical descendents of his work.

Paul and I had many long talks about life in general, our society, ski racing which both of us thought we'd left for good and the purpose and potential of both photography and writing. Paul and his refuge were cherished and nutritious aspects of a decadent and despairing time in Berkeley. Paul had a goal—to learn the craft and art of photography and then do something fulfilling with them, and, of course, to have a good life in the process. I wanted to learn to write but any goals I had were limited to getting through the day and having a place to sleep that night and trying to understand the havoc I had made of my life—physically, mentally, spiritually, emotionally and socially. I didn't think of it for several years, but I have long been informed and amused that within a few years of our street/student time (mine being a self-imposed depression, adrift and physically hobbled) in Berkeley, California we had each made significant contributions to different aspects of the world we loved most: skiing. Such thoughts bring to mind one of my favorite Winston Churchill quotes, "If you are going through hell, keep going."

I regularly shared a Berkeley bed that belonged to 'B', a young woman I'd known and dated a few times at the University of Nevada. B was from Berkeley and had come back home to attend law school. She was intelligent, funny and ambitious and often sabotaged by insecurities and dark personal demons that appeared at unexpected times and made my own ogres seem like rays of sunshine. We studied and talked and ate together and sometimes drank too much and regretted it in the morning. B's hospitality and companionship were appreciated and in some ways comfortable, but neither of us could handle more than a few days together, and I would find other sleeping quarters with friends or, last resort, the Oakland world of flop houses via a 25 cent public bus ride.

These establishments were the least expensive sleeping quarters I've ever known. I don't remember the price but it couldn't have been more than a dollar or two a night. Usually, 4 to 10 single beds in a room and I was always the youngest by some 30 years. On one of my first visits a kind, old, mostly toothless gentleman noticed that I put my shoes under my bed and my clothes upon them and instructed me to take them all to bed with me to avoid them being stolen by one of my roommates. He assured me that would eventually happen. From then on my flop house night bed companions were my clothes, shoes and whatever bag I carried with toiletries and spare clothes. The sounds of old men wheezing, coughing, snoring and sometimes moaning and talking to their nightmares were the melodies of my flophouse nights in Oakland.

A few times I camped on the Oakland couch of Aunt Motie who had shared an apartment with my mother and Aunt Minnie during WWII and whose son, Peter, was my childhood friend. Motie was nice to me and gave good counsel on how to deal with my mother, and her gratitude to have some immediate connection with her family was larger than her obvious disapproval with my life, lifestyle and the person I was becoming. Still, I enjoyed my visits and I believe she did as well.

Another favorite Berkeley couch belonged to Sherry, a friend from Reno attending college in the Bay Area who was engaged to a high school classmate of mine. He later broke off their relationship and I thought he was insane to lose her. Sherry was stunningly beautiful, intelligent, fun, witty and a fine conversationalist. Being me, I privately lusted after her, but we were only good friends and fun loving comrades and I relished those times I stayed with her. We once took a bus together from Oakland to Reno and drank rum and talked all the way to Reno where her fiancé picked us up and then drove me to my parent's home and I remember having the greener grass thought as they drove away of what a lucky couple they were.

Funk showed up just after a skiing trip to New Zealand. He was staying with some friends in Sausalito across the bay and with his usual good cheer and intense spirit encouraged me to think about skiing and the mountains and a body that worked and to pay attention to other people's judgments without letting them determine mine. Funk was a beautiful friend and wise in matters of the spirit if not the material ways of the world. Follow your own heart and instincts, not those of others, he said. His brief visit was a sliver of light and cheer that remained after he moved on, as he always did.

B's mother showed up at her daughter's apartment a couple of times while I was there. She was obviously and understandably wary of my presence but we chatted and seemed to get along. One of the things we talked about was the journals in which I wrote most days and I remember telling her the practice was good for a writer and a record of the day for future reference. I had some old journals with me and at some point B's mother somehow came to the apartment when no one was home and the door open and found my journals which I had stupidly left there in a pack and took them. Or so B told me. I phoned B's mother and complained and she hung up on me. I went to the office of a Berkeley lawyer and asked for advice that I had very little money to pay for. He must have been amused but he was kind and made a phone call to the mother and then advised me that unless I had some sort of proof that even filing a complaint with the police department would be fruitless. Still, I persisted and the lawyer accommodated me as best he could and we threatened court action for several months. I implored B to get my journals back and phoned the mother again and she hung up again and I never saw my journals again. It has always rankled, but only in the writing of this memoir more than 50 years later did it occur to me that B herself was the more likely thief. At the time, the thought a friend would read my private journals without permission did not cross my mind. Naïve does not fully describe such a mindset, but, as mentioned, it was not the best or clearest thinking period of my life. The journals included some tales B had related about her work as a prostitute in San Francisco to finance her first year of law school, and it seems likely now that she read them and decided such stories should not be loose in the world of the written word. Who could blame her? Years later the fine American writer Joan Didion wrote: "My only advantage as a reporter is that I am so physically small, so temperamentally unobtrusive, and so neurotically inarticulate that people tend to forget that my presence runs counter to their best interests. And it always does. That is one last thing to remember: writers are always selling somebody out." Nevertheless, it was a bummer to lose those journals and I've always wondered what became of them and if they still exist. They weren't just pieces of paper with scribbles on them, but, rather, an integral material and spiritual part of my education as a writer and my progress (and sometimes, alas, regression) as a human being, and losing them, especially in such a way was like a piece of my own flesh being literally and figuratively ripped off.

In the first entry of the first journal after the theft of the old ones I wrote: "October 15, 1961: "The diary was (as this one will be in time) a guide, a notebook, a history, an expression. It will be used to learn from and in order to write better. Like everything worthwhile to a person, it is interesting and enjoyable <u>to that person</u>. This is for no one else and I put here that anyone else who ever reads further than this line is a sneak, a peeping Tom and a thief. Those are truths; my own feelings on such a matter are somewhat more descriptive. The other diary which was exactly like this one except the cover was red was a friend, a long time companion, an attempt by myself at truth and expression, an object of pride to me like my skiing used to be and still is in a different way, it was a part of me, of my life, at a crucial point, of the secret feelings within which no one wants anyone else to see. It also contained my entire output of poetry. That was only fifteen poems, but when fifteen is the all then fifteen is a hell of a lot.

"When it was gone I was hurt…..When it was gone I was angry…..When it was gone I felt disgust and revulsion…..When the diary was gone I felt shame"

The stolen journals were another part of a life that seemed to be falling apart piece by piece from a young man hanging onto darkness instead of seeking the light, an operating description of someone (me) who has said "fuck it" to an engaged life. I was feeling sorry for myself, more, feeling I *deserved* to feel sorry for myself, wallowing in self-pity (a redundancy) and retreating inside to a private hell of my own making. On the outside I certainly wasn't retreating. My regular diet of the most filling and cheapest food available washed down lots of beer, combined with recreational exercise rather than training exercise, had added more pounds to my body than it ever had before or since. I weighed about 185 pounds, some 20 pounds overweight. There is no accurate method of determining the weight of a fat head, but mine was assuredly more than 20 pounds over healthy, clear thinking. And my heart was heaviest of all. I had let go of hope.

And then one night about three months after the nail came out the top of my foot, it changed.

In early November I was walking down a hallway after a class and thinking of the flophouse and sounds of sad old men snoring and yelling into the night, whether or not I should have a couple of beers before I decided whether to go to B's or hop the bus to Oakland and what I was going to do with myself the next day. I noticed a poster on the wall advertising a ski film by Sverre Engen, one of three Norwegian brothers who immigrated to America in the 1930s and became icons of 20th century American skiing. The movie was showing in an adjacent building and was just about to begin. I immediately decided that a skiing film was better than a couple of beers and hurried to its showing. The film had just started when I entered the small, dark, half-filled auditorium. I picked a seat at the end of an empty row in the rear and settled in to the enjoyment of images of skiing, skiers, mountains and the stories Sverre told about them. It was wonderful entertainment and nourishment for the soul, and just watching the film made me happy in a way I had not felt in several months. I could feel my muscles mimicking what the skiers on screen were doing, telling me in the language of life that I *belonged* to the world shown on that screen and not to the streets and couches and flophouses and bars and self-absorbed sorrows of the Berkeley world I'd been drowning in for the past few months. Halfway through, the film became a surrealistic experience for me, one I later related to my first LSD experience four years later when I had a vision of Marcel Duchamp's "Nude Descending A Staircase" and understood it for the first time (I know Duchamp is considered a Dada, Cubist and Modernist painter, but I associate the word 'surreal' with both my ski film in Berkeley 1961 and LSD at Tahoe 1965 experiences). Most ski films feature at some point in the narration the most spectacular fall. After all, falling is an integral part of the world of skiing, and skiing is both microcosm and metaphor for all of human life. Every filmmaker knows the audience will like seeing the scariest, most dramatic fall. The film switched to the U.S. National Downhill Championships in Alta, Utah in January of 1960, almost two years earlier. And, sure enough, here I came, the model for the most spectacular fall of the evening on a screen in an auditorium at the University of California in Berkeley. It was, indeed, an impressive fall and bad enough to make any viewer happy it wasn't him or her. But it had happened to me, and I was shocked and amazed to see it on film. It looked as bad as it had felt two years earlier and I was flooded with memories both surreal and graphic, and, significantly, pragmatic as the leg broke and my life changed. On film I could see the primary technical skiing mistake that caused the fall and, as if it were happening in slow motion, the human failings that led to the mistake were clear to me if not to anyone else in the audience. It was a revelation. I had fucked up and in that instant I understood that fucking up was no reason (or excuse) for saying "fuck it" as I had been doing for the past few months. Human beings fall every day. That's part of the human condition, and the worst response to a fall is to say "fuck it" and not get back up. In that surreal instant I resolved to get back up and back on skis and back to the mountains and back to myself just as the film switched from the fall and the first people to gather around my inert form, unrecognizable with helmet and goggles, to close ups of my pain filled face in the toboggan with a splint on my leg, looking just like a young man who has fallen and injured himself and is not happy about it. Right then, someone in the front rows of the audience said, "That's Dorworth." Someone else said, "Yeah, it is."

At least two people in the audience knew me, and I did not want to see them, whoever they were, or, more accurately, I didn't want them to see me in the shape I was in, which I had just that minute truly seen for the first time. I got up and left the auditorium without watching the rest of the film and caught the first bus to Oakland. Instead of going to the flophouse or to have a couple of beers I went to the Greyhound Bus depot where Mom had worked during WWII and took the first bus to Reno. I slept peacefully for most of the ride through the night across the Sacramento Valley and up and over the Sierra and Donner Pass and down along the Truckee River to the city of my birth where I had decided to start life and living all over again. I went to my parents' house at 885 Akard Drive in the northwest section of town and had a long meeting. I told them I was going to put my life back on the track where it belonged, by which I meant moving back to Reno, returning to the university and finishing and returning to ski racing until it was over. I apologized for all the turmoil and heartache my marriage and divorce from Charlotte and leaving Scott had caused and would cause them as well as me and Charlotte and Scott, but there was nothing to be done about it. I stayed with Mom and Dad a few days and arranged to start back at the University of Nevada in January and I went up to the sand dunes on Mt. Rose highway and began the brutal task of getting my fat ass and abused body, psyche, mind and spirit back in shape.

For the next several weeks I commuted between Berkeley and Reno, usually by Greyhound bus, finished night classes, registered as a full-time student at Nevada for the next semester, managed to regain my old job with the Economics Department which I had left a year earlier in favor of Aspen (I know little about economics and never took an economics class, but I edited a department newsletter that was distributed throughout the state), skied as much as possible, worked out furiously, and slowly, so slowly, began to feel and think and act like the human being I once knew. Though I didn't expect or request it, my parents not surprisingly suggested that I live with them in the spare bedroom until I finished college, saving me the burden of rent. That was a bigger help than just the complimentary rent and it allowed me a great deal of additional freedom and saving of time and energy. In the truest sense, my parents and my four year old brother Louis were my friends who came through for me when it most was needed. Their home was a haven.

Friends both old and new welcomed me into the warmth of their community and were insulation against the coldness of those who I came to think of as 'false friends'. In due time, a couple of them warmed up, apologized for their animosity and we repaired our relationships. One of them, Nina Freedman, among my harshest critics and best of Charlotte's friends, went to work a few years later in the office of the U.S. Ski Team in Colorado and gained an appreciation of skiing as passion and path, more and other than a healthy recreation for the privileged. Nina contacted me after a stony silence of more than six years and became one of my most cherished friends until her death of cancer several years later.

I am reminded (again and again) of the lovely Haiku by Soseki (1275-1351):

What is your
Original Nature,
Snowman?

My journal of January 10, 1962 reads, "Skiing is my life and I must have been insane to even think of quitting it. That will not happen again." Ten weeks after walking out of the film in Berkeley and getting on the Greyhound bus to Reno I had sweated 20 pounds off my fat ass, belly and brain. In February I had my first win in a ski race in more than three years, the Silver Dollar Derby in Reno, which I'd won in 1955. I won the slalom and the combined and placed 2nd in the downhill to Ron Funk. At the awards ceremony when we were being presented with our lovely silver trophies, Funk held his up and proclaimed, "Here's to Dick and the restoration of a badly abused ego!" A month later I was 3rd in the National Four Event (downhill, slalom, jumping and cross country, and known as *Skimeister*) Championships. That spring I placed 2nd in the NCAA slalom championship and 3rd in the *Skimeister* and was named to the 1962 NCAA All-American Ski Team. In May I was named 'athlete of the month' by the Reno newspaper. These are not earth shattering accomplishments or laurels to hang a life upon and are not presented as such, but they were a long, long way from the depression streets of Berkeley, the flophouses of Oakland and my pathetic reaction to the normal vicissitudes of life, including the loss of friends and the scorn of loved ones, that culminated in saying (and meaning) "fuck it" and stumbling off the path for awhile.

Within two years of crawling back onto the only path for me and into that seat on the Greyhound bus to Reno I had earned a BA in English from the University of Nevada, set a world record for speed on skis and knew in my broken and intact bones that I was on my path through the mountains and would not leave it again, though there have been rest stops along the way. More than 50 years later the path has taken me to high and beautiful mountain peaks and deep and frightening valleys, through gentle and fragrant meadows, by lakes and streams, sometimes accompanied by the best of friends and comrades, sometimes alone. There have been three more marriages and divorces, five sons in all, and now nine grandchildren. No existence is entirely easy or without pain and change and evolution, but it seems to me that every person has his and her own path to follow in life and that much of the turmoil and suffering of humanity is a consequence of saying "fuck it" to that personal path.

Find your own only path and stay on it.

END

CPSIA information can be obtained
at www.ICGtesting.com
Printed in the USA
BVOW10s1507301017
499010BV00009B/123/P